Successful Expert Testimony

This book outlines the role of expert testimony in a trial, including explanations of methods, testing, and science, the legal process, and an overview of the roles of each player. In this, it details the expert witness's role in promoting effective, impactful courtroom testimony.

Succeeding as an expert witness requires a basic understanding of who and what experts are and what role they play in rendering their opinions within the courts. The new edition has been fully updated to present key information on the most vital functions the expert plays. This includes the deposition, a discussion of the dangers of false or unsupported testimony, adherence to scientific principles, and the direct and cross-examination testimony of expert witnesses. Each chapter includes key terms, review questions, and thought-provoking discussion questions for further consideration of the topics addressed. Given many recent high-profile cases and increasing incidents of misconduct, this edition focuses heavily on the role of ethics in expert testimony and forensic practice. Outlining established trial-tested tips, forensic scientist Max M. Houck and attorney Christine Funk update renowned lawyer Harold A. Feder's classic book.

This is an essential reference for forensic science students entering the work force—in labs and investigative positions—in addition to serving as a crucial resource for more experienced civil, private, and testifying experts in all disciplines.

Successful Expert Testimony

Sixth Edition

Max M. Houck, PhD, FRSC, Christine Funk, Esq,
and Harold A. Feder

CRC Press
Taylor & Francis Group
Boca Raton London New York

CRC Press is an imprint of the
Taylor & Francis Group, an **informa** business

Designed cover image: Getty Images (deepblue4you)

Sixth edition published 2026
by CRC Press
2385 NW Executive Center Drive, Suite 320, Boca Raton FL 33431

and by CRC Press
4 Park Square, Milton Park, Abingdon, Oxon, OX14 4RN

CRC Press is an imprint of Taylor & Francis Group, LLC

First edition published by Van Nostrand Reinhold 1990

Library of Congress Cataloging-in-Publication Data
Names: Houck, Max M. author | Funk, Christine author | Feder, Harold A. author
Title: Successful expert testimony / Max M. Houck, PhD, FRSC, Christine Funk, Esq, and Harold A. Feder.
Description: 6th edition. | Boca Raton, FL : CRC Press, 2026. | Previous edition: 2018. | Includes bibliographical references and index. |
Summary: "This book outlines the role of expert testimony in a trial, including explanations of methods, testing, and science, the legal process, and an overview of the roles of each player. In this, it details the expert witness's role in promoting effective, impactful courtroom testimony. Succeeding as an expert witness requires a basic understanding of who and what experts are and what role they play in rendering their opinions within the courts. The new edition has been fully updated to present key information on the most vital functions the expert plays. This includes the deposition, a discussion of the dangers of false or unsupported testimony, adherence to scientific principles, and the direct and cross-examination testimony of expert witnesses. Each chapter includes key terms, review questions, and thought-provoking discussion questions for further consideration of the topics addressed. Given many recent high-profile cases and increasing incidents of misconduct, this edition focuses heavily on the role of ethics in expert testimony and forensic practice. Outlining established trial-tested tips, forensic scientist Max M. Houck and attorney Christine Funk update renowned lawyer Harold A. Feder's classic book. This is an essential reference for forensic science students entering the work force-in labs and investigative positions-in addition to serving as a crucial resource for more experienced civil, private, and testifying experts in all disciplines"– Provided by publisher.
Identifiers: LCCN 2025050503 (print) | LCCN 2025050504 (ebook) | ISBN 9781041005759 hardback | ISBN 9781041005728 paperback | ISBN 9781003610540 ebook
Subjects: LCSH: Evidence, Expert–United States | Witnesses–United States Classification: LCC KF8961 .H68 2026 (print) | LCC KF8961 (ebook)
LC record available at https://lccn.loc.gov/2025050503
LC ebook record available at https://lccn.loc.gov/2025050504

ISBN: 9781041005759 (hbk)
ISBN: 9781041005728 (pbk)
ISBN: 9781003610540 (ebk)

DOI: 10.4324/9781003610540

Typeset in Minion
by Deanta Global Publishing Services, Chennai, India

Dedication

I'm dedicating this book to my parents for being so supportive of my education. I owe what I have attained to them. I am dedicating this book to Jay Siegel, my teacher, my mentor, my friend. His advice was invaluable over my career and I miss him more than he would know. This book is also dedicated to the narrow-minded, short-sighted, ignorant nitwits who irritate me, much as sand does oysters, to the point of productivity. I hope this is a pearl.

M.M.H.

To Jef, who believed in me from the beginning. For Madeleine, whose skepticism and inquiring mind give me hope for the next generation. And, finally, much gratitude to my co-editor, Max, whose willingness to include me on madcap adventures brings me great joy, expands my horizons, and generally makes me a better person for it.

C.F.

Contents

Authors

Dr. Max M. Houck is a forensic scientist and author with over 30 years of experience in laboratory casework, research, program leadership, and forensic policy. His casework includes the Branch Davidian investigation, the Pentagon attack on September 11, the UNABOMBER, the West Memphis Three, and the Toy Box Killer, among hundreds of others. As a physical scientist in the FBI's Laboratory Division and later as director of multiple forensic programs at the local and national level, Houck has worked across scientific and operational boundaries, including independent reviews of forensic failures and consultations with defense teams and innocence projects. He was among the early proponents of using business analytics in forensic laboratories, co-founding Project FORESIGHT and advancing the "business of forensics" as a professional research domain. Dr. Houck is one of the most published professionals in his field and his work is among the top two percent of legal and forensic medicine researchers in the U.S. In addition to publishing widely on forensic science methodology, management, and reform, Dr. Houck has served on advisory panels for the White House, the National Academies of Sciences, Interpol, the Royal Society, and NIST. He is Editor-in-Chief of *Forensic Science International: Synergy* and a member of multiple editorial boards including Nature *Scientific Reports* and *PLOS One*. A Fellow of the Royal Society of Chemistry and full member of Sigma Xi, Houck has appeared on Forensic Files, National Geographic, and History Channel. Houck is currently the Forensic Portfolio Innovator at Florida International University's Global Forensic and Justice Center, where he supports translational research, international collaborations, and professional education in forensic science.

Christine Funk started her career in the Minnesota Office of the Public Defender in 1994. In 1995, she was assigned her first forensic DNA case. Over the years, her forensic caseload expanded to include arson, broken babies, drug chemistry, forensic biology, bitemarks, as well as the study of false confessions and eyewitness identification in the context of complex litigation. In 2013, Funk moved to Washington, DC to become General Counsel for the Department of Forensic Sciences. In 2017, Funk returned to Minnesota where she writes about issues pertaining to the law and forensic science, provides representation to indigent clients, and consults with criminal justice stakeholders, as well as those writing about forensic science, from investigative pieces to movie scripts to a television pilot. Previously, Ms. Funk has served on the Legal Resource Committee for the Organization of Scientific Area Committees, the Board of the Minnesota Innocence Project, the Forensic Laboratory Advisory Board for the state of Minnesota, and the White House Sub-Committee to the Sub-Committee on Forensic Science in Education, Ethics, and Terminology.

Harold A. Feder (1932–1995) was a trial lawyer with 35 years of trial experience. Most of his cases involved the use of experts. Feder was a fellow of the college of Law Practice Management and the American Academy of Forensic Sciences, a member of the Association of Trial Lawyers of America, past president of the Colorado Trial Lawyers Association, and an active member of the American and Colorado Bar Associations. Feder wrote and lectured extensively on legal matters, including expert testimony, throughout the United States and Canada for over 20 years. He wrote *Succeeding as an Expert Witness* in 1991; the text was revised in 1993, 2000, 2008, and 2018.

Foreword by Peter Neufeld

What does it mean to succeed as an expert witness? Is success measured by whether the side that summoned you to the witness stand prevails at trial? By recommendations that you make a convincing presentation to judge and jury? By the size of the fee you command in the marketplace or the promotions and awards bestowed upon you in the public sector? My own belief is that none of these are benchmarks of success.

Forensic science and by extension, expert witnesses are at a crossroads. The extraordinary power of DNA to identify the guilty and exonerate the falsely accused is one factor driving the wave of new graduate programs and expansion of undergraduate departments in forensic science. But while DNA typing may be a "truth machine," all too frequently, the truth revealed in post-conviction DNA testing is that years earlier, less powerful (by today's methods) or misapplied forensic science had been presented at trial by the "successful" expert witness to secure what turned out to be a false conviction.

Television's fictionalization of crime scene investigation is so successful that the public seems to prefer crimes be investigated by technicians in white lab coats rather than by old fashioned gumshoes in rumpled, coffee-stained sport jackets. But is the forensic community's reliance on TV misplaced when the consortium of national forensic organizations parades the TV actors before Congress to lobby for crime lab funding?

Finally, the national mobilization to combat terrorism and defend the homeland lends urgency and patriotism to the justice system; the "righteousness" of the cause, however, may inadvertently compromise the integrity of the result. In the identification sciences, "matching" the suspect to the crime sample can help win the war on terror much the same as it played an important role in the war on crime. But, since experts utilize subjective human judgment, expectation and suggestion can influence outcome. Indeed, one lesson from the DNA post-conviction exonerations is that examiner and confirmation bias are involved in too many erroneous hair, toolmark, and bitemark inclusions, as well as mistaken findings of homicide and arson when the cause was ultimately proven to be accidental. In the aftermath of the 2004 terrorist attack on a commuter train in Spain, the FBI erroneously claimed that the fingerprint of an Oregon attorney with ties to the Islamic community, but no criminal record, "matched" a fingerprint found on a plastic bag containing detonators found near the Madrid crime scene. In the affidavit used to justify the arrest of the lawyer, the two FBI examiners swore they were 100 percent certain of the match. The Spanish police insisted that the FBI was wrong: An Algerian terrorist was ultimately linked to the fingerprint. Without the persistence of the Spanish police, the FBI would not have reconsidered its findings. One irony of any mismatch is that whenever an innocent man is falsely charged or convicted, the real criminal or terrorist remains at liberty to commit further acts of violence. Faulty forensics may wrongly exclude the factually guilty.

For years, the dominant argument for not regulating experts and forensic sciences was that every time an expert steps inside the courtroom, his work is vigorously peer reviewed and scrutinized by opposing counsel. A forensic scientist might occasionally make an error at the lab bench but the "crucible" of courtroom cross examination would expose it at trial. The "crucible," however, turned out to be utterly ineffective. In not one of the forensic science scandals of the last 20 years were the transgressions of experts revealed by counsel at trial.

Although forensic science is used most commonly in crimes of violence, and state courts receive almost 200 times more criminal prosecutions than federal courts, the overwhelming majority of challenges to the admissibility of expert testimony occur in civil cases in the federal system. When the courts in the 1990s moved from the *Frye* standard of admissibility to *Daubert*, they obligated judges to assume the role of "gatekeepers" and to exclude proffered scientific evidence unless it rested on scientifically valid reasoning and methodology. But since most criminal defense lawyers lack the training, skill, time, and money to mount credible challenges to speculative expert testimony, there is nothing for a gatekeeper to tend to. If the "crucible" is a fiction and the judicial system fails to provide meaningful controls to assure the integrity of the process, other remedies must be found further upstream.

Since an expert's conclusions should be predicated on first principles of science, one lesson of the DNA revolution is to require a basic research model that will test the core assumptions in each expert's discipline. Whereas DNA typing rests on a stable foundation extensively rooted in research well documented in the literature, many of the forensic sciences have not been put through the same paces. Basic research takes money and independence, more than agencies such as the National Institute of Justice can provide. Given the urgency of international developments and the success story of DNA, I think it likely that the federal government will rise to the occasion.

Another lesson of DNA typing is the necessity that other disciplines develop methods to provide meaningful frequencies of attributes and characteristics. New protocols need to be established to minimize unintentional bias. Essential principles of statistics, long overlooked by experts, need to be incorporated to substitute random match probabilities (the kind used routinely in DNA) for the uninformative and often misleading terms "match," "similar," and "inclusion." The published probabilities coupled with known error rates, based on external blind proficiency tests, could then be presented in court. The final downstream fix is to establish reasonable parameters for the content of expert reports and live testimony so as not to distort the probative value of the evidence. An expert's job is not simply to answer *all* the questions propounded by the attorneys on both sides. If a question is inherently misleading or scientifically irrelevant, the expert has an affirmative duty to alert the court and put the testimony back on track.

At the beginning of the twentieth century, a critical awareness and creative energy ignited a movement to modernize clinical laboratory medicine. One hundred years later, the time is right for a comparable transformation in forensic science. It is an exciting time for everyone who is part of this community. Succeed by being thoughtful and rigorous scientists. Succeed by being honest, objective, and ethical expert witnesses.

Peter Neufeld,
Partner, Neufeld Scheck & Brustin, LLP
New York, New York

Foreword by Radley Balko

Our justice system is an adversarial one. We allow each side in a dispute to present its case, and then we ask a jury of peers (or in some cases a judge) to determine which side prevails. In criminal cases, the state must prove a defendant's guilt beyond a reasonable doubt. In civil cases, a plaintiff must prevail by a preponderance of the evidence. To borrow from what Winston Churchill once said about democracy, this is a pretty terrible system, except for all of the others one might imagine.

The problem is that an adversarial system is heavily reliant on the power of persuasion, which isn't always the same thing as a pursuit of the truth. There are any number of factors that can drive the outcome of a jury or civil trial more than the facts of the case. Among them, who has the better attorney, who has more funding to hire investigators and experts. How sympathetic the jury finds the plaintiff or defendant, or even how likable a jury finds the opposing attorneys.

This book addresses the issue of expert witnesses. Ideally, expert witnesses give us more informed juries, which helps those juries arrive at the truth. Unfortunately, as with other aspects of the justice system, the adversarial system can aid expert witnesses in subverting the truth rather than facilitating it. For example, both prosecutors and defense attorneys have long complained about the so-called CSI Effect. The complaint is that the CBS franchise of TV shows about forensic analysts has conditioned jurors to expect far more of forensic expertise than forensics allows for. The complaint is that because of these shows and others like them, jurors today crave certainty from expert witnesses, and they're skeptical of anything short of that.

But a conscientious expert witness—particularly one whose expertise is in the hard sciences—tends to speak in terms of probability, not certainty. Prosecutors argue that this makes it more difficult for them to win convictions. (This complaint should be weighed against the fact that in most jurisdictions, prosecutors typically win 80–90 percent of the time.) On the other hand, defense attorneys argue that the CSI Effect makes jurors less skeptical of expert witnesses, particularly in areas of forensics that are presented to jurors as science but in which the methods of analysis haven't been subjected to scientific scrutiny—particularly in pattern-matching fields like bite mark analysis, shoeprint and tire tread analysis, and hair fiber analysis.

This brings up another way in which expert testimony can inhibit the search for truth in our justice system—the courts are not very good at distinguishing legitimate expertise from artifice. As the author of this book explains, the two prevailing cases that tend to govern how the courts assess the reliability of expertise— standards known as *Frye* and *Daubert*—are vague and too open to interpretation. But there's a more profound problem than even that—these rulings assigned the task of distinguishing valid expertise from charlatanism to judges.

Judges are trained to perform legal analysis, not scientific analysis. We wouldn't think of asking a judge to, say, come up with a game plan for an NFL team, or draw up the blueprints for a vacation home. Yet we regularly ask them to gauge the legitimacy of fields and experts in which the judges have no expertise at all, whether its forensics, complex accounting methods, psychology, or really any field that might be relevant in a criminal or civil trial. Typically, judges tend to first look to what other courts have done. That makes sense for someone trained in legal analysis because that's how our legal system tends to operate. Our system operates on precedent, which establishes reliability, predictability, and in most cases, some semblance of equality before the law (you are tried under the same rules, procedures, and policies as those before you).

But with expertise—especially scientific or science-ish expertise—this can present huge problems. Lawyers on all sides will tend to push the limits of expertise to get experts on the witness stand who will give testimony favorable to their side. If the other side challenges an expert's credibility, the judge will tend to look to previous courts for guidance. If there's no previous case law on point, judges tend to err on the side of letting the evidence in, and letting competing experts fight to persuade the jury.

This is misguided for several reasons. First, the fields for which you can find credentialed experts willing to take diametrically opposing opinions are the most subjective fields, and therefore tend to be those least scrutinized by the scientific community. For example, most cases involving bite mark evidence will feature expert witnesses on both sides, one or more of whom claim the bite mark matches or "includes" the defendant, and one or more of whom will claim the mark "excludes" the defendant, is indeterminate, or isn't a human bite mark at all.

The very fact that you can find experts willing to take such diametrically opposing opinions, for example, is a good indication that the field isn't scientifically reliable. Contrarily, you'll rarely find two experts who diametrically disagree over the number of common markers in two DNA profiles.

The other problem is that when you have competing experts, the set of skills it takes to persuade a jury is not necessarily the same set of skills it takes to be a careful and conscientious analyst. Juries can be persuaded by charisma, charm, and extraneous factors like how much an expert was paid. In criminal trials, they also tend to be skeptical of hired defense experts than of prosecution experts, who tend to be public employees. In fact, it may well be the case that the experts whom juries find most persuasive are the least scientific, given that, as previously explained, juries tend to crave the sort of certainty that science eschews.

These two mistaken ways with which judges often handle challenges to expert testimony—relying on what previous courts have ruled and, if there's no controlling case law, letting it all in and letting the jury sort it out—can then perpetuate an unfortunate feedback loop. Once a judge lets flawed expertise in, he creates a precedent, which future judges then rely on should that particular sort of expertise be challenged at a later date. Those future judges will rely on that ruling because most judges aren't likely to feel confident enough in their scientific expertise to overturn a precedent, or even to rule against the prevailing opinion from other judges in other jurisdictions. So the same mistakes get repeated in court after court, in jurisdiction after jurisdiction, not because of corruption or bias or maliciousness, but through passiveness and attrition.

This book is not about these flaws in the system I've just described. It isn't a polemic speculating about how those flaws happened, nor does it offer a prescription for how to fix them. If all expert witnesses followed the guidelines in this book, we'd still have a badly flawed system. But it would be less flawed than it is today. And expert testimony would be far less of a contributor to those flaws.

This is a book about how to be an honest, conscientious, and effective expert witness in spite of the regrettable shortcomings of our court system. It's about how to be transparent and forthright while navigating the legal landscape we have today, fraught as it can sometimes be. It's an instruction manual that, if followed, will at least give an expert witness the peace of mind to know that he or she is contributing to the search for truth, even if he or she has no choice but to operate in a system in which truth isn't always the priority.

Radley Balko
Journalist with the *Washington Post*, Author of
The Cadaver King and the Country Dentist:
A True Story of Injustice in the American South

Expert Witnesses
An Overview

1

Key Terms

Appellate Court
Burden of Proof
Civil Law
Complainant
Criminal Justice Process
Criminal Law
Depositions
Discovery
Expert
Federal Rule of Evidence
Grand Jury
Jargon
Jury of Peers
Lay Witness
Opinion
Petit Jury
Prosecutor's Information
Sixth Amendment of the Constitution of the United States
Technique
Work Product

> *It is the job of the law, and not science, to determine how science is to be used in the courts. But in another sense, our passivity has served both ourselves and the legal system poorly. It is the job of science, and not of law, to determine what is good science and what is not.*[1]

DOI: 10.4324/9781003610540-1

Introduction

Succeeding as an expert witness requires a basic understanding of who and what experts are. The U.S. legal system permits certain witnesses to render opinions based on data rather than merely reciting information. These opinions are sought to explain past, present, and future events. You may be or already are such a witness. In this book, you will learn why experts are unique and how they are selected to be a witness. An expert is a special, often controversial, position in our court and hearing procedures. Federal Rule of Evidence (FRE) 702[2] defines Testimony by Experts (the relevant FREs will be addressed in depth later in this book):

> A witness who is qualified as an expert by knowledge, skill, experience, training, or education may testify in the form of an opinion or otherwise if the proponent demonstrates to the court that it is more likely than not that:
>
> (a) the expert's scientific, technical, or other specialized knowledge will help the trier of fact to understand the evidence or to determine a fact in issue;
> (b) the testimony is based on sufficient facts or data;
> (c) the testimony is the product of reliable principles and methods; and
> (d) the expert's opinion reflects a reliable application of the principles and methods to the facts of the case.

This may seem to be a moot description—what's the big deal? Contrast FRE 702 with FRE 701. Opinion Testimony by Lay Witness:

> If a witness is not testifying as an expert, testimony in the form of an opinion is limited to one that is: (a) rationally based on the witness's perception; (b) helpful to clearly understanding the witness's testimony or to determining a fact in issue; and (c) not based on scientific, technical, or other specialized knowledge within the scope of Rule 702.

If you are guessing that a "lay witness" is everybody who does not possess "scientific, technical, or other specialized knowledge," you are correct. In religious organizations, all persons who are not a member of the clergy or of any monastic order are called "lay persons" and collectively comprise the laity. The phrase "lay person" is in the law, in the context of any specialized profession, to refer to those who are not members of that profession, in this case, scientists, technicians, or other specialists. If you are not one of these specific people, your testimony must be limited to any facts—what you have experienced with your five senses—or opinions drawn from those experiences.

Experts, on the other hand, are given a special license in testimony: They can testify about their professional opinion based on their education, training, and experience in a specific topic. A recent article[3] described an expert as:

> a person who, by virtue of training and experience, is able to do things the rest of us cannot. Experts are not only proficient in what they do, but are also smooth and efficient in the actions they take. Experts know a great many things and have tricks for applying these things to problems or tasks. Experts are good at plowing through irrelevant information in order to get at basic issues or actual problems. Experts are also good at recognizing problems as instances of ones with which they are familiar, generalizing alternative solutions and making good choices among the alternatives.

A few examples may help clarify the difference between laity and experts. Here are some statements of testimony designated either with L for laity or E for expert.

L: The man I saw leaving the bank was tall, about 6'.
E: The individual in the bank surveillance video is between 5'11" and 6'2" based on the photogrammetric calculations I performed.
L: The woman was wearing a blue sweater.
E: The victim's sweater was composed of dark-blue, round-polyester, and blue, bi-lobed acrylic fibers.
L: The guy looked like he was bleeding.
E: The victim has suffered a contusion, one and a half to two inches in diameter over his left orbital at the juncture of the left temporal bone.

It is not only the wording characteristic of a particular group (jargon), in this case, experts, that makes these examples expert testimony, it is the knowledge, skills, and expertise behind the statements and the interpretations that result from them. The expert's knowledge of methods (photogrammetry), skills at applying them (how did the expert determine the fibers were polyester and acrylic?), and expertise in applying them (practicing as a medical doctor) are what differentiate them from the average lay person. You might know a doctor or a scientist and perhaps understand what they do a bit better than others but you are not in a professional position to make scientific or medical judgments the way they do. It is not just knowing, however, that makes an expert. There is, philosophically, a real difference between a someone who knows something and an expert:

> A technique is a standard method that can be taught. It is a recipe that can be fully conveyed from one person to another. A recipe always lays down a

> certain number of steps which, if followed to the letter, ought to lead invariably to the end desired.[4]

Should something go wrong, the recipe does not provide the tools for remediating the problem. It takes a true understanding of how the technique works and why it works to correct problems or, in fact, to improve the technique. An internal corrective mechanism has been offered as one of the ways to distinguish science (astronomy, for example) from non-science (astrology).[5]

What kind of education and training make someone an expert? Table 1.1 lists a few of the extensive topics that may require expert testimony. As you can see, many of these topics would require a good deal of education and training for a sufficient level of expertise to offer professional opinions in a courtroom.

Our society reveres those with specialized knowledge. Those who abuse that reverence for personal or professional gain, however, are as equally despised as the real experts are admired. For this reason, FRE 702 adds that the expert's testimony must be "based upon sufficient facts or data" and be "the product of reliable principles and methods" as well as having been reliably applied. For this reason, federal courts advise their juries concerning expert witnesses:

> The Rules of Evidence ordinarily do not permit witnesses to testify as to opinions or conclusions. An exception to this rule exists as to those whom we call "expert witnesses." Witnesses who, by education and experience, have become expert in some art, science, profession, or calling, may state an opinion as to relevant and material matter, in which they profess to be expert, and may also state their reasons for the opinion.
>
> You should consider each expert opinion received in evidence in this case, and give it such weight as you may think it deserves. If you should decide that the opinion of an expert witness is not based upon sufficient education and experience, or if you should conclude that the reasons given in support of the opinion are not sound, or that the opinion is outweighed by other evidence, you may disregard the opinion entirely.[6]

It is a hallmark of the U.S. justice system that, although they cannot testify the way experts can, the "laity" do make up the juries and have the final say in the case being tried.

History of Experts in Trials

Expert scientific witnesses have a long history of service to the courts. The modern expert witness was a specific creation of the late eighteenth century but the birthing was awkward and contentious. As Golan says, the expert

Table 1.1 A few of the issues that may require expert testimony.

Accounting	Fraud
Actuarial evaluations	Grievance procedures
Administrative law	Handwriting analysis
Air, soil, and water quality and contamination	Health or zoning code violations
Application of federal regulations	Immigration issues
Appraisals	Juvenile matters
Appropriateness of warrant and warrantless searches	Labor laws
	Land use regulations
Aquifer and watershed sources	Lost economic opportunity
Arson	Materials testing
Assessing damages	Mine safety
Assessment of causation	Motorized vehicle collision and dysfunction
Banking or business activity	Network security
Banking practices and legal requirements	Odontology
Blood pattern analysis	Patent, copyright, and trademark
Boundary disputes and title defects	Pathology
Causes of fire, flood, or other casualty	Personal injury of all types
Chemistry	Photography-videography
Child custody and visitation matters	Pornography issues
Child or spousal abuse	Propriety of claim procedures and damages
Clean-up procedures and costs	Psychiatric and psychological evaluations
Construction defects	Questioned documents
Contract meaning and interpretation	Questions of wrongful termination
Crime scene reconstruction	Revocation of professional licenses
Criminology	Safe working conditions
Customs matters	Securities regulation and violation
Damages	Shoe prints-tire tracks
Digital evidence	Source of mineral specimens
Discrimination	Surgical procedure
DNA	Taxation
Domestic relations	Toxicology
Drugs	Trace evidence
Dynamics of machinery	Value of property for tax purposes
Employment compensation	Value of statutory benefits
Environmental and ecological damage	Wages, hours, and conditions of employment
Explosives	Workers compensation
Fingerprints	
Firearms and toolmarks	

witness was "a freak in the new adversarial world, an incompatible and inharmonious, yet indispensable and influential, figure in the modern adversarial courtroom."[7] At the beginning of the eighteenth century, an English court would have been recognizable to our modern eyes but only barely. The attorneys were marginally involved, the judge was an active participant and questioned the witnesses, and the accused represented themselves. By the end of the century, the judge was reduced to a neutral referee, the attorneys had taken control of the trial process and were the stars of the courts, and the process had taken on the adversarial approach used today. Scientists in that time were considered to be gentlemen and members of an elite, honor-bound guild who put their reputation first and finances second. Perhaps this is why scientists were allowed to testify in proceedings that did not personally involve them during a time when even the slightest personal interest in a legal matter disqualified someone as a witness. Scientists were perceived to be independent disinterested men of learning who were above the petty squabbles of those in the courts. The experts could, therefore, be counted on to provide and explain impartial objective facts that—although beyond the knowledge of the public—were central to the resolution of the legal dispute. Some of these perceptions carry over into our modern view of the scientist but we also know that scientists are only too human: they can make mistakes, lie, and even profit thereby. The adversarial nature of the courts played to these weaknesses and lead to a loss of reputation for scientists:

> The growing judicial recognition of their status as a special class of witnesses was not all good news for men of science. It may have underlined their critical importance for the judicial process, but at the same time it also perpetuated their marginalization within this process. In moving across professional and institutional boundaries, from the exclusivity of their lecture theaters, workshop, laboratories, and societies to the public courtroom, men of science hoped to present there laws that were not controlled by human whim. Instead, they found themselves manipulated as mere tools in the hands of the lawyers … As witnesses, they found themselves isolated in the witness box, away from the decision-making process. Browbeaten and set against each other, they found that their standard strategies for generating credibility and agreement were unsuitable for the adversarial heat of the courtroom. The result was a continuous parade of leading men of science zealously contradicting each other from the witness stand, a parade that cast serious doubts on their integrity and on their science in the eyes of the legal profession and the public.[8]

In the twentieth century, as the sciences developed from intricate hobbies to defined disciplines of study, so too did the reputation of expert scientific witnesses in the courts. It was no longer enough for a witness to declare their expert status, they had to demonstrate it through generally accepted practices used by other scientists in that field. The judge became the arbiter of experts and legal decisions (*U.S. v Frye*, specifically) assisted in that task. The *Frye* decision, which will be discussed in more detail later, held that the expert must have suitable credentials to offer the evidence and the evidence itself must "be sufficiently established to have gained general acceptance in the particular field in which it belongs." This shift from the person to the process heralded a new way for the legal system to treat science in its midst.

Post-World War II, the scope of the science offered in courts expanded as did the judges' responsibility to make sure that it was solid and reputable science and not quackery. By the 1970s, Frye was the standard by which all proffered scientific testimony was measured. During the 1970s, FREs, the requirements for using evidence in federal courts, were codified but they made no mention of *Frye*. Instead, the FRE offered Rule 702, which was broad and inclusive not to mention vague; what, for example, constituted "scientific, technical, or other specialized knowledge"? The courts intended for this to be sorted out by the experts and attorneys and determined by the judges.

STILL SPEAKING TRUTH: WILMER SOUDER'S 1954 ADVICE TO SCIENTIFIC WITNESSES

In 1954, physicist Wilmer Souder, a pioneer of forensic sciences at the National Bureau of Standards (now the National Institute of Standards and Technology, NIST), offered timeless advice to scientific experts testifying in court. In his article "Effective Testimony for Scientific Witnesses," Souder emphasized that scientists entering the courtroom leave behind the comfort of technical jargon and familiar peers. Their audience now is a jury of laypeople, whose understanding and ultimately whose verdict depends on clear, honest, and relatable explanations.

Souder's advice still rings true: Know your qualifications but don't oversell them. Present your methods and conclusions plainly, and always speak to the jury, not over their heads. Avoid opinions disguised as guesses, and resist the temptation to impress with complexity. "You must be the eyes for the jury," he wrote, "not the brains." Let the evidence do the work.

He also warned that experts do not operate in a vacuum; legal procedures, courtroom customs, and adversarial strategies all shape the expert's experience. Attorneys may be unfamiliar with the science, but they are skilled at identifying weak explanations. Judges enforce rules that scientists may find strange, but they must be respected. Above all, Souder urged humility. Being correct is not enough; the expert must also be comprehensible and credible under pressure.

Seven decades later, the tools may have changed, but the mission remains the same: Communicate clearly, testify truthfully, and never underestimate the jury's ability to understand the science, if you communicate it well.

Civil and Criminal Cases

Criminal law is the body of statutory and common law that deals with crime and the legal punishment of criminal offenses. "Criminal offenses" generally means actions that are counter to the good of society. This differs from civil law in that civil actions are disputes between two parties that are not of significant public concern; "civil law" also is used to describe all law outside of the criminal law context. Criminal law has been seen as a system of regulating the behavior of individuals and groups in relation to societal norms whereas civil law is aimed primarily at the relationship between private individuals and their rights and obligations under the law. Experts are useful in both kinds of legal cases but the archetypal forensic scientist who works for a law enforcement agency will work almost exclusively on criminal cases. Private experts face an entirely separate set of additional challenges.[9]

The Criminal Justice Process

The criminal justice process begins with an alleged crime. An accusation is made (by the person aggrieved, the complainant), which is investigated by law enforcement officers, acting as representatives of the government. A formal complaint, also called an indictment, is presented to a group of citizens, called a grand jury,[10] who determine if enough evidence exists for a criminal trial. If so, the indictment is filed with a court in the appropriate jurisdiction. Grand juries do not exist outside the United States and are not universal within it (Connecticut and Pennsylvania do not use grand jury indictments); each state that uses them has its own set of grand jury procedures. Many states use a prosecutor's information as a means of formally charging the accused of a crime. A prosecutor's information details the nature and the circumstances of the charges and is a formal criminal charge filed with the court. It is based on information derived from the initial investigation.

The interests of the state are represented by a prosecuting attorney, while the interests of the defendant are represented by their defense attorney or by the defendant, acting as their own attorney. The Sixth Amendment of the Constitution of the United States guarantees a criminal defendant:

- The right to a speedy and public trial, in both state and federal courts, by an impartial jury of the State and district wherein the crime was committed (a "jury of peers")
- The right to be informed of the nature and cause of the accusation
- The right to be confronted with the witnesses against him (this is where expert witnesses play a role)

- Compulsory process for obtaining witnesses in his favor (the subpoena)
- And the assistance of Counsel for his defence (Public Defenders, if the accused cannot afford counsel)

While the specific process varies according to the local law, the process culminates with a jury trial (as required by the Sixth Amendment), followed by mandatory or discretionary appeals to higher courts.

The prosecution must prove beyond a reasonable doubt that the defendant is guilty of the crime charged; this is called the burden of proof. The prosecution presents its case first and may call witnesses and present other evidence against the defendant. After the prosecution has presented its case, the defense may move to dismiss the case if there is insufficient evidence or present its case and call witnesses. All witnesses may be cross-examined by the opposing side. After both sides have presented their cases and made closing arguments, the judge gives the jury legal instructions and they adjourn to deliberate in private. The jury must unanimously agree on a verdict of guilty or not guilty. If a defendant is found guilty, sentencing (punishment) follows, often at a separate hearing after the prosecution, defense, and court have developed information based on which the judge will determine a sentence. As with the guilt phase, the burden is on the prosecution to prove its case, and the defendant is entitled to take the stand in his or her own defense, and may call witnesses and present evidence.

After sentencing, the defendant may appeal the ruling to a higher court. An appellate court ("appellate" is the adjectival form of "appeal") is a court that hears cases in which a lower court—either a trial court or a lower-level appellate court—has already made a decision but in which at least one party to the action wants to challenge this ruling. The challenge is based upon some legal grounds, such as errors of law, fact, or due process. American appellate courts do not retry the case; they only examine the record of the proceedings in the lower court to determine if errors were made that require a new trial, re-sentencing, or a complete discharge of the defendant, as is mandated by the circumstances.

Discovery and Deposition

Discovery is the pretrial phase in a lawsuit in which each party can request documents and other evidence from other parties or can compel the production of evidence by using a subpoena or through other discovery devices, such as depositions. Anything that is relevant is available for the other party to request, as long as it is not privileged or otherwise protected. Relevance is defined as anything more or less likely to prove a fact that affects the outcome of the claim. It does not have to be admissible in court as long as it could reasonably lead to admissible evidence. Discovery, however, does not mean everything is automatically turned over. The court may adjust the limits of discovery on the amount of material requested if it determines that the discovery sought is overly burdensome, redundant, unnecessary, or disproportionately difficult to produce with respect to the importance of the case or specific issue. Also protected are tangible (and some intangible) items created in anticipation of the litigation (so-called work product; for example, a memorandum from an attorney outlining his strategy in the case). Protecting work product is considered in the interest of justice because discovery of such work product would expose an attorney's complete legal strategy before trial. Experts whose opinions may be presented at trial are discoverable, but discovery is limited with experts who are not likely to testify during trial. Any material legally privileged (attorney-client, doctor-patient, etc.) also is exempt from discovery.

One of the main tools in the attorney's arsenal is the deposition. A deposition is evidence given under oath and recorded for use in court at a later date; in the U.S., depositions are taken outside of a courtroom. The chief value of a deposition, as with any discovery proceeding, is to give all parties in a case a fair preview of the evidence so that a "level playing field" is achieved and no surprises occur in trial (these used to be called "Perry Mason Moments," after the lawyer character in Erle Stanley Gardner's novels). In the event a witness is unavailable for trial, his deposition testimony may be read before the jury and made part of the record in the case, with the same legal force as live testimony. It is crucial for the expert witness to prepare for depositions just as they would a court testimony—in some states, depositions can be offered into evidence even if the witness is available! In any case, one party can use a deposition to impeach (or contradict) the witness's testimony in open court. While depositions may be more common in civil cases, some jurisdictions routinely use them (Florida, for example).

What you say in a deposition may come back to haunt you on the stand. Some depositions are videotaped, in anticipation of the unavailability of a witness at trial, so that if necessary the videotape may be played for the judge and jury. A deposition is designed to accomplish certain specific objectives:

- Gather information
- Uncover inconsistencies in testimony
- Document statements, processes, and work product
- Assess your ability as a witness

The examination is usually done by opposing counsel, with few if any questions by your sponsoring attorney. The setting is generally informal, scheduled in advance, and conducted in the presence of a certified court reporter; recording by video is common. You may also assist the examining attorney at deposition of opposing experts by assessing their qualifications, capabilities, and framing questions for them. Before your deposition, you should review the following:

- Technical and fact data from the case
- Your scientific and technical materials
- Pleadings on file in the case
- Products of discovery, such as interrogatories, document production, and depositions
- Standard scientific works relevant to the subject
- Appropriate legal authorities

Agreement of counsel or court approval is usually necessary before you may be deposed. The pleadings must show that the information sought by deposition cannot be obtained by other traditional and less expensive means of discovery.[11] Depositions may be taken either for discovery or in lieu of testimony in court because you are beyond the jurisdictional limits of the court's subpoena power.

As an expert, you should play an important role in pleadings and discovery preparation. You may be called on to word technical parts of a pleading. You can also review discovery requests and responses for completeness and technical consistency. In some cases, you can help uncover a body of technical data, forms, procedures, protocol, notes, and research materials. It is often essential that you participate at this stage to ensure that requisite scientific and technical information is available before deposition. Preparing for deposition should be a joint effort between you and the attorney.

Preparation for Trial

Before trial, you will assist in preparing exhibits and demonstrative charts, tests, and documents. Any demonstration must be tested before the trial or hearing. Trial exhibits should be shown to opposing counsel in advance of trial, and either stipulation or court order approval should be obtained. These are easy ways to guarantee the admissibility of a key chart, exhibit, document, or demonstration. It is proper for you to ask the attorney calling you if these details have been satisfied. Nothing can be as disappointing as preparing costly demonstrations or exhibits that are rejected at trial because of inaccuracy or lack of foundation. Exhibits and demonstrations must be accurate and technically correct. Note that demonstrative evidence may be excluded because it is deemed "prejudicial," meaning that its value as evidence is outweighed by its shock value or inflammatory nature. Color photographs of mutilated bodies or even technically accurate autopsies are often considered too emotionally-disturbing to be useful as evidence.

Unnecessary exhibits and testimony should be eliminated before trial. Your calculations should be rechecked. Data should be summarized whenever possible: Have the raw data available in the courtroom but refer to summaries of voluminous documents or material. New Rules of Evidence allow this use of summary data.[12] The large amount of raw material you have evaluated before trial can enhance the weight of testimony. The data from which summaries are made must in all cases be available for examination by opposing counsel. Good practice dictates that such information be made available well before trial and be in court for opposition examination.

Preparation for trial is somewhat different from preparation for deposition. The attorney should explain to you the objectives of testimony and describe the physical setting of the hearing room in detail, including positioning of the parties, the attorneys, and the dispute resolution forum.

At Trial

First, the attorney who subpoenaed you will try to have you qualified as an expert by the court. In essence, you present your education, training, and experience as qualifications for your right to speak authoritatively on the evidence you examined. This will be covered in greater detail in a later chapter.

Think of the people involved in a trial: The judge, the attorneys, the jurors, you. Of all those who play a role in the proceedings, how many are under sworn oath to tell the truth? Just you, the witness. This is not to say that anyone will lie to you with intent, but they could. It may be an omission by accident as well, but it's best to remember you—the witness—are the only one who has sworn to be truthful.

During the trial, you should be aware of the importance of careful testimony, particularly the hazard of inconsistent testimony between deposition and trial. You are admonished to tell the truth and to prepare for deposition or trial testimony by reviewing the facts of the case and your work effort. You should not lose your temper. Speak slowly, clearly, and naturally. If you are familiar with the process, you will not fear the examining attorney or the setting. You must answer only the questions asked, never volunteering information beyond the scope of the question presented. You need not have an answer for every question. Avoid arguing with or second-guessing examining counsel. If you make a mistake, correct it as soon as possible. If a negative or apparently damaging fact or omission has been elicited, admit it and move on quickly. To fence, hedge, argue, equivocate, or become angry only exposes you to further cross-examination and a resultant loss of credibility.

Testimony in court, deposition, or hearing should never be turned into a joke. Exaggeration, underestimation, or overestimation are all indications of unwary and ill-prepared witnesses. You must translate technical terms into common, understandable language at every opportunity. Your demeanor and behavior before, during, and after testimony should be the subject of care. Conversations with opposing parties, attorneys, and jurors must be avoided.

At trial your testimony will be divided into five main parts:

1. Voir dire, presenting your qualifications as an expert to render opinion testimony
2. Direct Testimony
3. Cross Examination
4. Redirect and re-cross-examinations
5. The judge retaining or excusing you as a witness

Conclusion

You as an expert, because of your knowledge training and experience, are allowed to render opinions about scientific or technical matters during the trial processes. You may be called on to assist in all phases of investigation, preparation, discovery, and trial of contested matters. Your role is to transmit specialized information and knowledge to the fact finder (judge or jury). In many cases, your effectiveness will help determine the outcome. Although your primary role is to provide your direct testimony, anticipation of cross-examination will facilitate your persuasive response. You should prepare for cross-examination and frame a strategy for answering vulnerable areas. Above all else, be truthful and answer the questions asked of you. Testimony may not always be pleasant[13] but it is an integral part of modern courtroom procedures.

Review Questions

1. How is an expert different from a lay witness? What can they do?
2. What is jargon?
3. When were the Federal Rules of Evidence enacted?
4. What is a technique? Is it the same as a method?
5. What is the difference between criminal law and civil law? What needs do they serve in the criminal justice process?
6. Who or what is a complainant?

7. What is a grand jury? Is it different from a petit jury?
8. What does the Sixth Amendment of the Constitution of the United States provide?
9. What is discovery?
10. What is a deposition? Is it different from a trial? Explain.

Discussion Questions

1. Is the grand jury process necessary? Why or why not?
2. Why is the Sixth Amendment important to you as an expert?
3. Why is the discovery process necessary? Often, discovery is not reciprocal and the defense does not have to divulge all of its information. Why do you think this is so?

Notes

1. Thornton, J., "Courts of Law v. Courts of Science: A Forensic Scientist's Reaction to Daubert," *Shepard's Expert and Scientific Evidence Quarterly*, 3 (1994), pp. 475–485, p. 476.
2. Federal Rule of Evidence (FRE) 702 was amended on December 1, 2023. The amendments address common misinterpretations and misapplications of Rule 702 by trial courts.
3. Johnson, P.E., Johnson, M.G. and Little, R.K., "Expertise in Trial Advocacy: Some Considerations for Inquiry into Its Nature and Development," *Campbell Law Review*, 7 (1984), p. 119.
4. Barrett, W., *The Illusion of Technique* (Garden City, NJ: Anchor/Doubleday Press, 1979), p. 22.
5. Kuhn, T., *The Structure of Scientific Revolutions* (University of Chicago Press, 1962).
6. Devitt, E.J. and Blackmar, C.B., *Federal Jury Practice and Instructions*, 3rd ed., Vol. 1 (West Publishing Company, 1977), §15.22, p. 482.
7. Golan, T., *Laws of Men and Laws of Nature: The History of Scientific Expert Testimony in England and America* (Cambridge, MA: Harvard University Press, 2004), p. 7.
8. Golan, T., *Laws of Men and Laws of Nature: The History of Scientific Expert Testimony in England and America* (Cambridge, MA: Harvard University Press, 2004), p. 54.
9. Hamilton, R., *The Expert Witness Marketing Book* (Clearwater, FL: Expert Communications, 2003).
10. Grand juries have more members than a trial, or petit, jury, hence the name.
11. This is particularly true under the Federal Rules of Civil Procedure and in states that have adopted similar rules. See, for example, Rule 26(b)(4), Federal Rules of Civil Procedure.

12. See, for example, FRE 1006.
13. 78 percent of the students in one of Houck's court testimony classes said they would rather have their hands slammed in a car door twice than have to testify again. The instructor was one of the highest rated by students in that program, so it is, in fact, a reflection on the testimonial process.

Methods, Testing, and Science

2

Key Terms

Falsifiability
Paradigms
Normal science
Scientific revolution
Hypotheses
Accreditation
American Society of Crime Laboratory Directors Laboratory Accreditation Board (ASCLD-LAB)
International Standards Organization (ISO)
American Board of Criminalistics (ABC)
ASTM, International
Certified reference material (CRM)
National Institute of Standards and Technology (NIST)

Introduction

Typically, a case begins with an event involving people, places, events, and objects. In most cases, you will become acquainted with those four fundamental elements. The combination of people, places, and things in a chance moment of time creates a crime, accident, injury, damage, or event (or absence of an event) that may precipitate the need for forensic services. The unique correlation of people, places, and things within a defined time frame constitutes the unusual element of almost every forensic case. Carl Jung referred to it as synchronicity. It is this incidental nature of the forensic realm that separates it from the non-forensic sciences, which generally call for well thought out, carefully planned experiments. Suppose you investigate a body found in a van. In the wheel wells and the tire treads of the van you find pieces of what appear to be soil. Upon further inspection, you identify the particles as bits of roofing tile. It is doubtful your laboratory has a prepared protocol for the analysis of roofing tiles.

What methods, then, are best applied? What standards exist? How do you source the tiles to the house or location they came from, manufacturer

DOI: 10.4324/9781003610540-2

or production batch? Given the "incidental synchronicity," to coin a phrase, of forensic science, how do we know what to do in any given case?

Accreditation, Certification, and Standardization

Accreditation is the process by which a laboratory establishes a baseline of minimum safeguards showing its services are offered with a certain degree of quality, integrity, and assurance that consistent procedures are applied in each case. The accreditation process is extensive, rigorous, and demanding for the laboratory that undertakes it. The laboratory and its staff first undergo a comprehensive self-study and evaluation with a long checklist of requirements. Once the laboratory implements the procedures called for on the checklist, the laboratory then applies for accreditation. The accrediting agency sends out a team to perform an on-site evaluation by trained members of the accrediting body. If the laboratory passes evaluation, it becomes accredited. Accreditation is maintained through periodic review, both internal and external. Given all of this, it is important to remember that accreditation is the least a laboratory can do about quality; it says nothing about the competence of the individual forensic scientists who work there. Being accredited means the laboratory meets certain *minimum criteria* for the facilities, security, training, equipment, quality assurance and control, and other essentials.

Certification is a voluntary process of peer review by which a practitioner is recognized as having attained the professional qualifications necessary to practice in one or more disciplines of forensic science. In most jurisdictions, certification of individual analysts is not required at this time. The American Board of Criminalistics is one entity that offers certification and specialty certifications in forensic biology, drug chemistry, fire debris analysis, and trace evidence. Other entities or professional agencies offer certification for their sciences, such as the American Society of Forensic Questioned Document Examiners, the International Association of Identification, and the Society of Forensic Toxicologists.

Standardization plays a major role in helping laboratories become accredited. "Standard" is a word that has at least two very different meanings in forensic science. A standard can take two forms. It can be a written standard much like a very specific recipe that has to be followed exactly to get a result considered acceptable. The ASTM, International (American Society for Testing and Materials, International) has long published standards for a wide variety of sciences, including forensic science (in Volume 14.02). These standards are written by groups of experts in the field who come to agreement on the acceptable way to perform a certain analysis. More recently, the Organization of Scientific Area Committee for Forensic Science (OSAC) has established a registry for forensic science standards for forensic science disciplines.

A standard can also be a physical thing, such as a sample of pure copper. Physical standards like this are called reference materials because scientists refer to them when analyzing other samples—if a specimen is 99.999 percent pure copper, then its properties are known exactly, as is how it ought to react in an experiment. If the reference material has been tested extensively by many methods, it can be issued as a certified reference material (CRM). CRMs come with certificates guaranteeing their purity or quality. The National Institute of Standards and Technology (NIST) is the main agency of the U.S. government that issues CRMs.

WHY ARGUING IS ESSENTIAL IN FORENSIC SCIENCE

Science advances through argument; so does justice. In forensic science education, it's easy to focus on methods, results, and conclusions but what often gets lost is how we know what we know. That's where argumentation comes in. Argumentation means constructing claims, evaluating evidence, anticipating counterarguments, and refining explanations. It's not about fighting; it's about thinking critically and communicating clearly.

The same skills that scientists use to vet a theory, like questioning assumptions, weighing alternative explanations, identifying weak links, are central to the courtroom. Forensic experts are expected not only to present their conclusions but also to explain the reasoning behind them and respond to challenges. And juries? They don't just need facts, they need arguments they can understand and trust.

Research shows students learn science better when they're encouraged to debate ideas. That applies doubly in forensic science, where the ability to defend methods, question findings, and explain uncertainty isn't just educational, it's professional. In fact, it's what separates the technician from the expert. Learning to argue is learning to think like a forensic scientist.

Osborne, J. 2010. Arguing to learn in science: The role of collaborative, critical discourse, ***Science***, 328(5977), pp. 463–466.

What Is Science?

One of the most important people in the history of science was a lawyer: Sir Francis Bacon, who rose to be Lord Chancellor of England during the reign of King James I, wrote the book *Novum Organum*. In it, Bacon details his theory of the scientific method: The scientist should be a disinterested observer of the world with a clear, unbiased mind free from preconceptions that might influence his understanding. With sufficient observations, patterns will emerge out of the data and the scientist can make specific statements as well as generalizations about nature.This may sound straightforward, but attempts to apply this method reveal its shortcomings. No serious scientific thinker or philosopher, nor your average lay person, accepts Bacon's theory that science works through the collection of unbiased observations. Everything about the way people do science—the words, the instrumentation, the procedures—is framed by preconceived ideas and our experiences about how the world works. It is impossible to make observations about the world without knowing what is and is not worth observing. People are constantly filtering their new experiences and observations through those things they have already experienced. Complete objectivity is impossible.

With that understanding, Sir Karl Popper, a noted philosopher, proposed that all science begins under a prejudice, a theory, a hypothesis—in short, an idea from a specific viewpoint. Popper worked from the premise that a theory can never be proved by agreement with observation—you do not know if the next observation will support or refute it—but it can be proved wrong by disagreement. This asymmetric nature of science makes it unique among ways of knowing about the world: Good ideas can be proven wrong to make way for even better ideas. Popper called this aspect of science falsifiability, the idea that a statement must be able to be proven false if it is to be considered scientific. Popper's view of constant testing to disprove statements biased by the preconceived notions of scientists replaced Bacon's view of the disinterested observer.

Science is a complex endeavor and Popper's ideas do not completely describe science any more than Bacon's did. While it may be impossible to prove a theory true, it is almost just as difficult to prove one absolutely false by Popper's methods. The trouble lies in distilling a falsifiable statement from a theory; additional assumptions that are not covered by the idea or theory itself must always be made. If the statement is shown to be false, we may not know if it was one of the basic assumptions, additional assumptions, or the theory itself that is at fault. This confounds the issue and clouds what the scientist thinks he has discovered.

Defining science is not a simple matter. It takes a great deal of hard work to develop a new theory that agrees with the entirety of what is already known in any area of science. Popper's falsifiability, scientists attacking a theory at its weakest point to bring it down, is simply not the way people explore the world. Thomas Kuhn, a physicist by education and training who later became a historian and philosopher of science, offered a new way of thinking about science. Kuhn wrote that science involves paradigms, consensual understandings of how the world works. Within a given paradigm, scientists add information, ideas, and methods that steadily accumulate and reinforce their understanding of the world. This is what Kuhn calls normal science. With time, contradictions and observations that are difficult to explain under the current paradigm are encountered. These difficulties are set aside as oddities or anomalies so as not to endanger the status quo of the paradigm. Eventually, enough of these difficulties accumulate and the paradigm can no longer be supported. When this happens, Kuhn maintains that a scientific revolution ensues that dismantles the old paradigm and replaces it with a new paradigm. The shift from Newtonian to Einsteinian physics is a good example of such a revolution.

Kuhn's main point is that while the central issues of theories are tested—and some are falsified—the daily business of science is not to overturn its central concepts. If a theory makes novel and unexpected predictions, and those predictions are verified by experiments that reveal new and useful or interesting phenomena, then the chances that the theory is correct are greatly enhanced. However, science does undergo startling changes of perspective that lead to new and, invariably, better ways of understanding the world. Thus, science does not proceed smoothly and incrementally, but it is one of the few areas of human endeavor that is truly progressive. Falsifiability is not the only criterion for what science is. The scientific debate is very different from what happens in a court of law, but just as in the law, it is crucial that every idea receive the most vigorous possible advocacy, just in case it might be right.

What Constitutes Science?

In a courtroom, the simple question "Is this science?" can have enormous consequences. In forensic anthropology and related disciplines, the admissibility of expert testimony often hinges on whether a method or opinion meets legal standards for scientific reliability. But determining what qualifies as "science" is not always straightforward. Science is built on a foundation of theory, testable hypotheses, empirical observation, and constant revision. It aims not at certainty, but at the best available explanation supported by evidence and subject to change. This open-ended process of inquiry contrasts sharply with the goals of the legal system, which values finality, clear outcomes, and procedural fairness. In law, evidence must be persuasive enough to meet specific burdens of proof ("beyond a reasonable doubt" in criminal cases) even if it cannot meet the rigorous standards of scientific proof.

This disconnect can lead to trouble in court. A case in Virginia where a forensic anthropologist's testimony about the healing time of a child's bone fracture was excluded, is a good case in point. Although based on experience and research, the court ruled the testimony lacked a known error rate, a sufficient theoretical foundation, or "general acceptance" in the field. This outcome reflects a broader tension: Science rarely provides 100 percent certainty, while the courtroom often demands it. Yet science and the law also share common ground. Both use abductive reasoning, inferring the best explanation from incomplete information, and both must weigh competing interpretations of past events. The forensic scientist, like a juror, assesses the plausibility of hypotheses based on available evidence. Increasingly, probabilistic models such as Bayesian inference are being used to help bridge the gap between scientific reasoning and legal decision-making by quantifying uncertainty and relevance.

WHAT IS ABDUCTIVE REASONING?

Abductive reasoning is the process of forming the most plausible explanation from incomplete or uncertain evidence. It's sometimes called "inference to the best explanation." Imagine walking into a kitchen and seeing a broken glass on the floor with milk spilled everywhere. You didn't see what happened … but you might reasonably infer that your cat knocked the glass over. That's abduction: Using available clues to reconstruct what probably occurred.

In forensic science and the courtroom, abductive reasoning is fundamental. Neither the scientist nor the jury sees the crime happen. Both must piece together events from traces left behind. While science tests these inferences with further data and experiments, the courtroom weighs them against legal standards like "reasonable doubt." Abductive reasoning doesn't guarantee certainty, but it helps us navigate ambiguity. It's the reasoning behind expert conclusions and the bridge between science and the law.

The case demonstrates that forensic anthropologists, and by extension all forensic scientists, must do more than rely on expertise. They must clearly articulate the theoretical basis of their conclusions, cite error rates where possible, and provide statistical support when interpreting evidence. Doing so not only helps courts understand the science, it also strengthens the standing of the discipline itself. Ultimately, what constitutes science in the legal context is not just about methods and results; it is about transparency, rigor, and the ability to explain how those methods lead to a reliable conclusion under scrutiny. Without that foundation, even good science can be misinterpreted or excluded.

In the language of science, the particular questions to be tested are called hypotheses. Suppose textile fibers are found on the bed where a victim has been sexually assaulted. Do the textile fibers come from the victim's environment, the suspect's, or somewhere else? The hypothesis could be framed as, "A significant difference exists between the questioned textile fibers and the known textile fibers from the suspect's sweater." Notice that the hypothesis is formed as a neutral statement that can be either proved or disproved. After the hypothesis has been stated, the forensic scientist seeks to collect data that sheds light on the hypothesis. Known textile fibers from the suspect's sweater are compared with those from the scene, the victim, and others who are known to have reasonably potentially left textile fibers at the scene. All relevant data will be collected without regard to whether it favors the hypothesis. Once collected, the data will be carefully examined to determine what value it has in proving or disproving the hypothesis; this is its probative value. If the questioned textile fibers are analytically indistinguishable from the known textile fibers, then the hypothesis is rejected. The scientist could then conclude that the questioned textile fibers could have come from the suspect's sweater.

But suppose that most of the data suggest that the suspect is the one that left the textile fibers there, but there is not enough data to associate the textile fibers to him. It cannot be said that the hypothesis has been disproved (there are some similarities), but neither can it be said that it has been proved (some differences exist, but are they significant?). Although it would be beneficial to prove unequivocally that someone is or is not the source of evidence, (and this cannot be stressed enough) *very little evidence can be individualized*. The important thing to note here is that evidence analysis proceeds by forming many hypotheses and perhaps rejecting some as the investigation progresses.

Formulating a Working Hypothesis

After investigation and testing have yielded findings, the next step is to formulate a working hypothesis. The following hypothetical case shows how this might be done by the lawyers. Suppose the prosecution's hypothesis is that the defendant, charged with burglary, was the perpetrator of the burglary. The prosecution further hypothesizes the defendant is the seller of the stolen goods taken during the burglary, to the state's prime prosecution witness. The state's forensic fiber expert was able to analyze and establish that fibers analytically indistinguishable to known fibers from the stolen materials were in both the defendant's van and his home closet. This evidence strongly supported the prosecution's hypothesis that the defendant at some time was in possession of the stolen materials. But does it speak at all to whether the defendant committed the burglary and theft of the goods originally?

The defense's hypothesis was that the defendant was not the perpetrator, however offered no exculpatory evidence. Do the fibers alone negate the defense hypothesis? No. However, in the American justice system, the defendant has no obligation to prove anything. Rather, the burden of proof is entirely on the state. Thus, the question becomes, how significant are the fibers? What if the defense presents evidence there was no burglary, but rather, the defendant purchased the items from the owner, who later claimed, falsely, to have been burgled? What if the defendant provides a legitimate bill of sale for the purchase of similar, not stolen items?

The hypotheses of the lawyers may change, but, in this example, the hypothesis of the scientist remains constant. The theories of prosecution and defense have no bearing on the analysis of the fibers themselves. At the end of the day, the jury, as the trier of fact, determines the relevance of any given piece of evidence.

Use of a Standard Protocol

One essential investigating device is the standard protocol, where one exists. Comparison of that standard to your facts may reveal significant oversights or discrepancies. Many scientific, technical, and professional tasks are the subject of standard protocols. Your task as an investigating forensic witness is to locate that standard protocol and examine the case against it. Your conclusion may be that standard procedures were followed. Or you may determine that important steps were omitted. This can provide valuable information about the reliability and reproducibility of the results of the examination.

Additionally, failure to follow a protocol raises questions about potential civil or criminal culpability, depending on the facts and circumstances of a given case. Accredited forensic laboratories are required to have written protocols for the analyses they conduct, either ones they have written themselves or ones they have adopted from standards agencies, such as ASTM or ISO. Of course, these written protocols are only of value if they are followed. When deviations of the protocol occur, this should be documented completely, including why the protocol was deviated from, how the protocol was deviated from, etc.

Published Method

The scientific literature is a peer-reviewed source of information, methods, and results. When faced with questions on analysis or with particular samples, it is important for a scientist to review the literature on that topic. The scientific literature includes:

- Professional and technical journals
- Dissertations
- Commercial literature
- Manufacturers' product bulletins
- External validation studies
- Relevant test procedures
- Internal validation studies
- Other experimental studies

The expert's own files, including lecture notes, laboratory tests, reports prepared in prior forensic cases, prior depositions in similar cases, and prior testimony, may also be useful. The literature survey will vary in each case, however, depending on the field and the specific case. Your own library of reports, surveys, articles, lecture notes, and testimony transcripts should be studied in preparation for testimony.

Towards Admissibility

To increase the probability that your tests, experiments, demonstrations, and models will be admissible, follow the below steps:

- Be thoroughly familiar with the facts of the case (Note: This is not a reference to the "case" in the civil or criminal justice system. This is a reference to the scientist's "case" in the laboratory)
- Have available accurate measurements
- Be familiar with the progression of events that occurred in the laboratory, including decisions made regarding order of testing, the type and nature of testing performed, etc.

- Use the same materials that were involved in the event under study
- Meticulously track your tests or experimental steps
- Record the tests or experimental events carefully
- Make your demonstrations substantially similar to the actual events in issue
- Make your models to a precise scale
- Detail all findings, both positive and negative
- Where no protocol exists, do sufficient research and consultation with peers and supervisors to establish that the test or experimental procedure is scientifically and technically recognized as authoritative
- When preparing an exhibit, consult with counsel, where appropriate, to ensure the best posture for tendered admissibility

Be aware that all decisions made, to test or not to test, to test in one way instead of another, etc., are subject to questioning by the lawyers. Consequently, your decisions about testing should be well documented.

Destructive testing raises additional challenges because of the risk entailed in destruction of real evidence. Every effort must be made to be conservative of evidence—each item is unique and irreplaceable. Non-destructive testing options should be exhausted before any evidence is consumed in analysis. This is not just a nice idea but an ethical imperative. In addition, depending on the jurisdiction and the posture of the case, destructive testing, without permission from the prosecution, defense, or the court, could result in a determination that test results are inadmissible. The analyst or the lab may also be subject to sanctions for such destructive testing without permission. Consequently, it is critical each analyst is familiar with current lab policy about destructive testing.

Test results may determine the outcome of a case. Unless the test or demonstration is adequately founded, there may be serious problems concerning admissibility. Always take careful steps to ensure adequate foundation for tests, demonstrations, or models by following generally accepted scientific methods, the protocols in place within the laboratory, documenting each step of the procedure, and limiting conclusions to those supported by science. A passing understanding of the Rules of Evidence also helps the expert prepare scientific, technical, and professional testimony.[1]

Conclusion

Investigation is the process by which one gathers the data on which one's opinions and reports will be based. Many ideas and lists can be used to make the process more efficient. Plan your work and work your plan. Learn from others, review the literature, and conduct tests and research to verify that methods work. As you gather the facts, give consideration to graphic displays that will help you later present the material in an understandable and effective way. Constantly strive to translate your findings into non-technical layman language. The most complete casework will be of little importance if the result cannot be relayed in a clear, effective, and understandable way.

Review Questions

1. What is falsifiability?
2. What is a paradigm?
3. What is normal science?
4. What is a scientific revolution?
5. What is a hypothesis?
6. What is accreditation?
7. What is ASTM, International?
8. What is a certified reference material?

Discussion Questions

1. Describe the roles of ASTM, ISO, laboratory accreditation, and NIST. How do they matter to you as an expert who testifies?
2. Why is it important to be able to define science? How would you define it?
3. What is the importance of considering hypotheses other than the one(s) presented to you?

Note

1. Cautionary note: The writers of fictional television have about as much legal education as your average forensic scientist. A scientist should not rely on the same for knowledge of the Rules of Evidence.

The Players 3

Key Terms

Bench trial
Circuit court
Competence
Contempt of court
Defense attorney
District court judge
Juror
Jury
Jury trial
Justices of the peace
Mistrial
Narratives
Paradigm shift
Prosecutor
Public defender
Rhetoric
Small claims court
Supreme Court of the United States
U.S. Court of Appeals
U.S. District Court
Voir dire

Introduction

Court proceedings are not a frivolous matter. After all, peoples' lives and livelihoods are at stake. In civil court, typically it is money that is at stake. In criminal court, it is liberty, including both potential jail or prison time, as well as supervision on probation or parole, that is at stake. Despite these high stakes, it may seem, however, that some participants, particularly the attorneys, enjoy "the challenge of the hunt." As an expert witness, it can be daunting to have attorneys wax rhetorically while you are required to "just answer the question." Additionally, as lawyers are not, as a general rule, scientifically

DOI: 10.4324/9781003610540-3

trained, difficulty may lie in the inartful presentation of the questions presented by the lawyers. A trial is not a game, but gamesmanship, including skill, strategy, and long-term planning, is involved. Those who might think it a game do not understand the roles the participants must play, and that includes themselves.

This chapter discusses the roles of those professionals involved in the trial process: The attorneys, the judge, the jury, and, finally, the expert.

The Attorney's Role

Attorneys in the U.S. justice system are advocates, relics of the champions of jousting fields of the past. As such, their duty is to put forward a set of facts and proofs that support their position—in short, a narrative. Occasionally, zeal for the cause may shade professional and intellectual independence. As a starting point, it is not improper for the advocate to give you a wish list stating the most desirable conclusions from the attorney's viewpoint. This does not mean, however, that you must support that view. In fact, wish list aside, your scientifically-based conclusions will inform the attorney of the actual (rather than desired) state of affairs. Your integrity, reputation, and personal and professional self-esteem, in addition to the prohibitions against perjury, require that the conclusions you reach and opinions you espouse be supportable based on the available body of facts and operative knowledge. Follow the scientific method regardless of the path it forces you to take. Experts' findings assist the attorney first in evaluating the strength or weakness of their case. Even where an expert isn't called to testify at trial, or the case doesn't go to trial, the expert plays a valuable role.

The role of the attorney is to represent their client, be it "The People" or a person. A prosecutor's goal in a trial is to seek justice. A defense attorney's goal in trial is to vigorously defend the constitutional rights of the defendant. Both want to win. A lawyer (prosecutor or defender) does this by creating narratives, verbal accounts of events intended to prove or disprove a certain point—what Welsh has called a "strong representation."[1] The arguments of the attorneys are not, in themselves, evidence. Rather, the arguments presented to the jury are offered as a guide to the jury. Jurors are called on to rely on their own recollection of the witnesses' testimony in coming to their decision. Attorneys, when arguing their client's case, "subordinate the facts to a conclusion that makes a difference," and that conclusion "purports to review all the facts … because, in the opinion of the person making the representation, the facts when considered rightly all point in one direction." An adversarial position is presupposed in this view in that one must take a stance to argue a particular point: Either the defendant is or is not guilty of the crime of which he is accused. Legal narratives are often complex and specific. Defenses can include, but are not limited to:

- The defendant didn't commit the crime
- No crime was committed
- The defendant committed the crime but has a defense such as self defense, defense of others, prevention of a felony, mental illness, entrapment, etc.

The activities in question in a legal case are often unseen by unbiased viewers. In eighteenth-century England, the diminishing respect for personal testimony (people do lie, after all) and the growing use of circumstantial evidence[2] led to the predominance of the attorney as a representational narrator. "Objective" physical evidence—in conjunction with the enhanced respect of scientists as a professional class—became the new weapon of the trial lawyer. Ironically, the evidence became almost as important as the trial itself. The narratives became more complex, requiring explanation of the myriad facts and interpretations of those facts involved in the expert evidence. The accused was no longer capable of defending himself:

> People need not go about telling their stories and hoping for the best; instead, the stories should be managed with a careful view to the consequences. This management obviously takes ability and experience and, above all, hard work and therefore can best be left to professionals—and a professional representation is thought to be an impressive performance in it own right.[3]

It is not a game, but it is a presentation of selected facts intended to prove or disprove an assertion, and it is best left to someone skilled in that art: The attorney.

When people criticize attorneys for being "shifty" or "liars," they miss the point of what attorneys are supposed to do: Provide arguments for or against a particular proposition. Arguments are rhetoric—the art or technique of persuasion, usually in public or legal settings—and it is the method of the lawyer; words are their weapons, grammar their tactics, and arguments their strategy. If you were accused of a crime you did not commit or were a victim of a crime, you would want an attorney who presents the strongest possible case in your favor. The rules of the courtroom are different from those in the law or the laboratory. Scientists will often complain that lawyers will "bend the facts" to suit their needs, ignoring the essential difference between lawyers and scientists: Lawyers use facts rhetorically as building blocks in an argument; scientists use facts objectively as verifiable observations. Crossing those boundaries carries a price: One commentator has suggested the central flaw in Microsoft's anti-monopoly legal strategy was that it handled the case like an engineer would have and it cost them.[4]

In the United States, in most states, lawyers are required to complete a college degree as well as attend and complete law school, which typically is an additional three years of study. Upon completion of the requisite education, in most states and under most circumstances, people must also pass a bar exam before becoming licensed to practice law. Criminal prosecutors are employed by city, county, district, state, or federal government. While prosecutors may be employed either full- or part-time, while engaged in prosecution, they act on behalf of the government that employs them.

Criminal defense attorneys work on behalf of people charged with, or being investigated for, crimes. They may work for a law firm, they may be self-employed, or they may work as a public defender. Public defenders represent people who cannot otherwise afford an attorney. Public defense systems vary from state to state, and sometimes even within a given state. In some states, public defenders are state employees. In other states, each county operates an independent system of public defense. In still other states, courts appoint lawyers to represent indigent clients on a case by case basis. The public defense system exists because the right to counsel is a constitutional guarantee under the Sixth Amendment. In *Gideon v. Wainwright*, the Supreme Court of the United States clarified court-appointed counsel is covered by the Sixth Amendment for defendants who are "indigent," or cannot afford to hire their own counsel. Regardless of whether the defense attorney is paid by the client, the client's parents, or the government, the defense attorney works on behalf of the client.

The Courts

The courts constitute the judicial branch of government. There are several different types of trial courts. The U.S. district courts are the general trial courts of the U.S. federal court system. Both civil and criminal cases are filed in district court. Each federal judicial district has at least one courthouse, if not more. The formal name is "the United States District Court for [name of the district]," for example, "the United States District Court for the Central District of California" (see Figure 3.1). The U.S. courts of appeals (also called circuit courts) are the intermediate appellate courts in the federal system, which are required to hear all appeals from the district courts within their federal judicial circuit. In state court systems, there is usually a similar system of intermediate appeals, and a high court for the state. The U.S. circuit

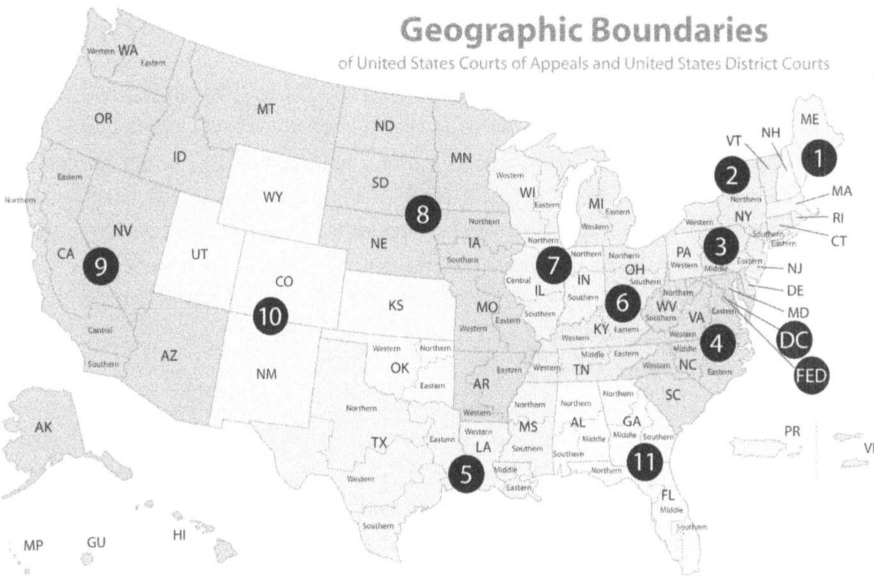

Figure 3.1 The district courts of the United States. Source: U.S. Government.

courts were U.S. federal courts established in each federal judicial district. These circuit courts exercised both original and appellate jurisdiction from 1789 to 1912. The original jurisdiction of the U.S. circuit courts is now exercised by the U.S. district courts, and their appellate jurisdiction is now exercised by the U.S. courts of appeals. The "circuit courts" were officially known as United States circuit courts of appeals from 1894, until their name was changed to United States courts of appeals in 1947. The term circuit refers to earlier times when a judge and several attorneys would ride on horseback through a jurisdiction (making a circuit), hearing cases at multiple locations.

The Supreme Court of the United States is the highest judicial body in the United States and is the only part of the judicial branch made explicit in the U.S. Constitution. It has the highest appellate authority among both the state and federal courts that Congress may create—it is often referred to as the court of last resort. The court consists of nine justices nominated by the president and confirmed by the Senate.

Most forensic scientists who work for local or state jurisdictions will testify in a state court, which has jurisdiction over disputes with some connection to a state. The overwhelming majority of cases are heard in state courts. Cases are heard and evidence is presented at a trial in a courthouse typically in the county seat. A decision in a state court may be appealed (except for an acquittal in a criminal trial due to the Fifth Amendment protection against double jeopardy) and that decision will be reviewed by a state court of appeals. A state supreme court will sometimes hear appeals by those still unsatisfied. If this sounds vaguely familiar to the federal system, you are correct, but do not make the mistake of thinking the state courts are subordinate to the federal courts. State courts operate in a parallel way to federal courts and hold dominance in the arena of interpreting state laws. States also vary in their court structure and process. While Indiana has 177 superior courts, 90 circuit courts, 5 courts of appeals, and a supreme court, West Virginia has 31 circuit courts and a supreme court of appeals. Other states have no circuit courts, but rather refer to them as district courts. Experts are not expected to understand the varying intricacies of district versus circuit versus superior courts. They are, however, expected to arrive at the proper courthouse for testimony.

Criminal charges brought against a person fall into one of three main categories: Infractions (sometimes referred to as petty misdemeanors, depending on the jurisdiction), misdemeanors, and felonies. Infractions are the least serious crimes and include offenses like parking or speeding tickets and building code violations. Infractions typically are punishable with a fine. Misdemeanors are more serious than infractions and include violations such as petty theft, prostitution, vandalism, and trespassing. Conviction of a misdemeanor may involve jail time, as well as probation, classes, such as theft prevention classes, where appropriate, community service, and/or a fine. The most serious crimes, which are felonies, include assault, arson, burglary, robbery, murder, rape, and fraud. Some states classify felonies according to their seriousness, and the state's legislature typically determines the maximum punishment allowable for each felony. Imprisonment for more than a year is the punishment in some states, while the death penalty can be the punishment for felonies in others. Felons often face other sanctions, such as loss of voting rights (suffrage) and exclusion from certain kinds of jobs, ownership of firearms, and public office. Certain felons may also be required to register for some period of time, based on their offense. Finally, depending on the laws of the state, persons arrested or convicted of crimes may be subject to the collection of DNA samples, to be profiled and placed in the appropriate state or local database.

The Judge's Role

Judges are the leaders of the judiciary branch of government. Judges are to be impartial and not influenced by outside factors, such as political power, money, or fame. Judges are appointed or elected from among practicing attorneys. In rural areas, some states permit non-lawyers to serve as justices of the peace (judicial officers with limited authority, who preside over misdemeanors, traffic violations, etc.) or act as judges in small claims court (courts that hear private disputes where small amounts of money, typically $2500, or less, are at stake). After election or appointment, judges usually receive additional training.[5] Many are expected to attend regular judicial education and instruction sessions.

In their courtroom, the judge is the absolute authority. Phrases such as "If it please the court" and "Your Honor, may I approach the bench?" are not mere formalities—the request is conducted at the discretion of the judge. When a witness is finished testifying, he does not leave until the judge excuses him. A judge is addressed in writing as "The Honorable Jane Doe" or "Hon. Jane Doe," and in speech as "Judge" or "Judge Doe," or when presiding in court, "Your Honor."

In the U.S. legal system, in a jury trial, the jury decides questions of fact (guilt or innocence, for example) while the judge decides questions of law. Bench trials in the United States have a single judge who decides issues of both law and fact. Appeals are usually decided by a panel of judges.

One power that judges have is the power to punish any misconduct that takes place in the courtroom with a fine, imprisonment, or both. This is called contempt of court. The judge may also punish violations of the court's orders, after a hearing, when a violation takes place outside the courtroom. An expert witness who gets out of line by refusing to answer questions or does not appear in court when summoned may face contempt of court charges. Additionally, it is quite common for judges to grant motions requesting that the witnesses not discuss the case prior to their testimony. An expert who discusses the case with a fellow analyst, or another witness, risks a finding of contempt. Such conduct could also result in a mistrial.

The appeals process is the first line of defense for judicial oversight. Judges are people, after all, and judicial oversight is provided for cases where, apart from technical matters of the law, the judge may have exceeded or abused their authority, or was just plain wrong in his or her legal analysis. If the aggrieved does not feel satisfied with the result, they would then go to the state supreme court, if the state supreme court is willing to hear the case. Finally, in matters of national consequence, or involving federal protections, a party may request a hearing before the Supreme Court of the United States (which rules on whether it will hear a particular case).

The Jury's Role

A jury consists of six or twelve citizens who have been sworn to reach an impartial verdict in the case before the court. A person serving on a jury is a juror. Juries determine guilt and innocence and, in some instances, may render sentencing decisions. Those eligible to serve on a jury may never make it to trial; a vetting process, called voir dire,[6] enables the trial lawyers to ask questions of potential jurors to determine if they are biased about issues involved in the case, whether they have prior commitments that may prevent them from serving on a given case, or other legal considerations which may prevent service.

If a jury cannot reach a verdict in a sufficient amount of time (although no limit is set), a mistrial (cancellation of a trial prior to a verdict) may be declared. Depending on the basis of the mistrial, the defendant may or may not be tried a second time. The concept of a jury dates to the Magna Carta (1215), which provided English nobles and freemen the right to a trial by a panel of their peers, rather than solely on the decision of a king or other royalty.

The Expert's Role

The definition of an expert was provided previously: Someone who has specialized knowledge, skills, and education in an area of relevance to the trier of fact. The influence of the forensic expert in our lives today, helping shape not only future decisions but resolve present controversies over past events, assumes unusually vital proportions. But there are some philosophical impediments that the forensic witness must overcome before becoming truly effective.

- If forensic investigation suggests a result scientifically, technically, or factually irrefutable, why all the hassle? Why can't we experts gather around the table and resolve the dispute in a spirit of collegiality and fraternity?
- Why must I as an expert be subjected to rigorous cross-examination when the facts are so clear? After all, I am an expert, I have studied the facts, I am educated and trained in this area.
- How can there be an expert witness who studies the same facts and reaches a conclusion contrary to mine? The other expert must have had his opinion imposed upon him by opposing counsel.
- How can the attorney ask me to come to a specific conclusion in advance of my analysis? I refuse to have my profession insulted or my integrity challenged by an attorney who makes such a quantum leap.

These four misconceptions lie at the root of most fundamental misunderstandings between forensic witnesses and attorneys. It is in the very nature of the legal and scientific professions to be at odds, and a great deal of effort by both groups is required for a suitable and accurate outcome. The human aspect of being a scientist or an attorney cannot be forgotten. As Fourth Circuit Court Judge Russell Clawges has said, "If science were completely objective, we wouldn't need the experts."

Example of the Role of Scientist

The identification of human blood is an excellent parable of the way science may be (mis)applied in the courts. In the late 1800s, given a positive test for blood, many defense attorneys would simply argue that it was animal blood and offer a feasible alibi. At the time, few scientists thought that a test for human blood was possible, let alone reliable enough to send a person to jail or prison. Debate about tests for human blood had raged in forensic and pathology circles for nearly 50 years prior. This debate, and its effect on science in the courts, is instructive, as it offers an example of the role of science and its practitioners in the courts.

In 1877, it was well known that the size and shape of red blood cells ("red corpuscles" or erythrocytes) varied by species. Reptiles, birds, fish, and camels have oval erythrocytes, while mammals—except camels—have circular ones. Mammals' erythrocytes, including camels', are non-nucleated, meaning they do not have a membrane-bound subcellular that contains the cell's chromosomes, among other things. Thus, it is a relatively easy matter to use a microscope and determine if a fresh blood sample is mammalian or not (see Figure 3.2). The method espoused by many forensic specialists in the late 1880s was to measure the erythrocytes from a fresh sample and, based on an average diameter falling within a known range of variation, determine human from non-human blood.

Forensic samples, however, are rarely fresh. Erythrocytes are fragile and are susceptible to damage from environmental changes: Too wet and they pop, too dry and they shrivel. This made accurate measurement of the erythrocytes nearly impossible. No standard method existed, either. Instead, each expert had his own technique for performing the method. Microscopy at the time was becoming a discipline per se, and most microscopists, as we would now call them, hailed from many different disciplines.

Therefore, they were reluctant to gather under the banner of one leader, resolve their differences, and standardize the method. Arguments, some personal, abounded at professional society meetings and in the academic journals. The issue culminated in the Hayden trial of 1879 with two experts hotly

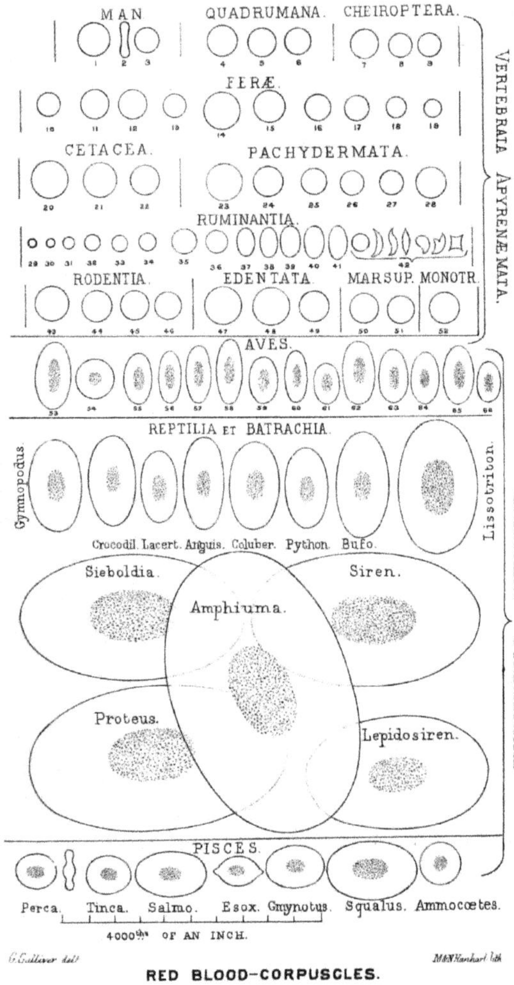

Figure 3.2 There is an immense size variation in vertebrate erythrocytes, as well as a correlation between cell and nucleus size. Mammalian erythrocytes, which do not contain nuclei, are considerably smaller than those of most other vertebrates. Reptiles, birds, fish, and camels have oval red blood cells (erythrocytes) while mammals—except camels—have circular ones. Mammals' erythrocytes, including camels, are non-nucleated, meaning they do not have a membrane-bound subcellular which contains the cell's chromosomes, among other things. It is a relatively easy matter to use a microscope and determine if a fresh blood sample is mammalian or not. Source: George Gulliver: Observations on the sizes and shapes of red corpuscles of the blood of vertebrates, with drawings of them to a uniform scale, and extended and revised tables of measurement. Proc Zool Soc London 1875:474–495. Open access at: biodiversitylibrary .org/page/28501724.

contesting the veracity of each other's testimony and intentions. The affair was accurately summed up by the *New York Times*:

> It is not necessary to impute dishonesty or mercenary motives to the eminent experts in medicine or other branches of science, whose disagreements put the minds of jurymen in a maze, instead of leading them into the light. But there are experts and experts, there are theories and theories, and there are even facts and facts, in every department of science or special knowledge, and lawyers can ingeniously make their selection, giving prominence to some and keeping others out of sight, and twisting and turning until the inexpert mind in the jury box is in danger of losing all faith in science as a witness.[7]

The camps were divided between the microscopists who thought the test faulty or limited, and the microscopists who felt it was better to offer some science to the courts. Ultimately, the scientists all agreed upon the facts about human and non-human erythrocytes—some mammals could be distinguished by their size and shape—but not about the meaning of those facts, what we would now call interpretation. Each microscopist saw the same types of samples but prepared them differently, measured them differently, and interpreted their significance differently. Despite this variance, measuring erythrocytes was held to be the premier forensic method for determining human blood until Paul Uhlenhuth's application of antisera to blood identification in 1901. Known as the serological test, it quickly replaced microscopic measurement in forensic science.

The points to remember from this historical example are numerous and important. First, scientific facts are open to interpretation; one set of facts may lead to a variety of conclusions. This variety of conclusions is resolved for scientists in laboratories, professional meetings, discussions, and academic journals. While it is true that experts involved in the same case might gather around a table and come to a consensus conclusion, they also might not. No consensus was achieved in the erythrocyte test. Rather, a completely new test trumped it. If agreement was not achieved after a decade or more of debate and publications, why would it happen in one particular trial? The perceived collegiality and fraternity of academia only goes so far. Scientists are human, and conflicts over scientific findings may persist for tens or hundreds of years.[8] Suspicion of influence by the attorney, or "scientific prostitution" by a greedy expert, need not be the cause of disparate findings.

Another point of interest to scientists is the supplanting of the erythrocyte test by the serological test; this could be seen as a minor example of what Thomas Kuhn calls a paradigm shift. Kuhn's concept was that science does not progress linearly, constantly accumulating new data and knowledge. Periodic revolutions—paradigm shifts—suddenly change the nature of scientific inquiry within a field. One of Kuhn's requirements is that the two theories are incommensurable (the understanding of one theory cannot be gained through a similar understanding of the other). The differences between the erythrocyte test and the serological test are not incommensurable (the size of the blood cell does not affect its antiseral properties), but you get the idea: The new test, because of its accuracy and precision, removed the old test from serious scientific consideration. Perhaps the shift was not a true revolution, but only a coup; nevertheless, it is easy to see how the same facts can be used honestly to render different conclusions.

These scientific debates are manifestly different from legal debates. The trial process, as messy and stressful as it may seem, has been considered the best means of arriving at a decision or resolution of conflict for hundreds of years. The mental obstacle of the question asked earlier, "Why must I as an expert be subjected to rigorous cross-examination when the facts are so clear?" is easily resolved when it is understood that the trial is a legal process and the expert witness is only one small part of that process. The expert assists the trier of fact in interpreting evidence that is beyond the knowledge of the average citizen who is eligible to serve on a jury. Further, the prosecutor carries the burden of proving each and every element of a case beyond a reasonable doubt. If work performed by an expert, or conclusions drawn by an expert, establish or support the existence of an element of the offense, the prosecutor must offer these facts as proof. This proof comes in the form of testimony. Similarly, the defense attorney's job is to make sure the defendant's constitutional rights are protected. If the expert has evidence which calls into doubt an element of the prosecutor's case, they must also offer that evidence to the jury in the form of testimony. Cross-examination is one method of ensuring all the relevant facts and information are made available to the trier of fact. Cross-examination may focus on the limits of the science, the assumptions that the scientist made, the basis for the conclusions drawn. It may consist of attacks on the science, the method, the scientist themselves. Cross-examination may focus on the relevance of the conclusions in light of various hypotheticals. Without knowing the attorney's theory of the case, it is difficult, if not impossible, to accurately guess the content of cross-examination ahead of time. Knowing that cross-examination is part of a trial helps to keep scientists clear about their actions. "Research performed for the purpose of litigation may afford no opportunity for true peer review … cross-examination can perform this function and can in itself be an incentive to perform good, transparent science."[9] The old saying "Pride goes before a fall" is appropriate here: If you are prepared, honest, and humble, you have nothing to fear from a cross-examination.

This leads to the last main point to be taken from the erythrocyte test story: What is useful in a trial may not be—and almost always is not—useful in discovering and expanding scientific knowledge. Trials deal with a specific conflict, have to be concluded in a reasonable amount of time, and need to have a definitive conclusion. An attorney, arguing one version of events, presupposes certain facts that will be useful to him. Was the suspect absolutely at the crime scene? If not, how much information points to his presence there—a lot? A little? Enough? The attorney needs to know what facts can be used and to what degree they favor his argument. The expert needs to make sure that the attorney does so accurately to the limits of the theories, science, and methods employed.

The Expert's Role in Court

It has been observed that jurors generally take to ordinary people, but they do not always like and trust experts. In other words, experts tend to depersonalize themselves through their methodology, vocabulary, or general demeanor. The end result is trial presentation by a robot-like creature who has become devoid of human attributes. The good news is, this situation is not inevitable. To be effective and credible, the expert witness must:

- Perform a thorough analysis
- Be personable, genuine, and natural
- Have an ability to teach
- Be generally competent
- Be believable
- Be able to persuade without advocacy
- Be prepared
- Be willing to weather controversy
- Demonstrate enthusiasm
- Listen to the questions presented
- Be willing to consider other alternatives, regardless of which attorney is asking the question or posing the hypothesis
- Admit when they are wrong

Without these qualities, the potential expert witness should not even contemplate stepping into the courtroom.

Thorough Analysis

As an expert, you should be aware that expert opinion testimony must be based on a reliable foundation and be relevant to the case at issue. You must be prepared to show that the professional, scientific, or technical premise on which you rely has a scientifically valid basis.

Ability to Teach

Testimony is an opportunity to teach. Think back to high school or college: Recall a favorite instructor or coach. Recollect the qualities that made you want to learn more from that person. Visualize those attributes, and emulate that person. A good teacher-expert is:

- Well-informed and prepared in their subject matter
- Apt to use demonstrative aids to enhance understanding
- Not intimidating or pompous
- Ready to use an example or analogy
- Questioning and humble
- Honest about gaps in his knowledge or information
- Friendly, human, and has a sense of humor
- Able to communicate complicated subjects in lay terms

Competence

Demonstrated ability and competence in the subject field is a mandatory element of effective expert testimony. Competence is demonstrated by thorough knowledge in the field; appropriate experience or credentials, as demonstrated by publications and presentations, as well as competency and proficiency tests, where appropriate; a currency of information; an ability to perform as well as teach; and an ability to recognize problems, elect alternatives, and make good choices among them. Competence is the demonstrated ability to do something at the expected level of performance.

Believability

You have to believe to be believable. You are not merely a mirror of the position established for you by an attorney. You are presented with a problem, afforded the opportunity to investigate and evaluate the facts, and asked to reach a supportable conclusion. Your conclusion was reached independently and is based upon available data. You are believable because you understand your science and your methods, and you can communicate those methods and science in a manner that jurors can understand. This provides confidence in what you are saying. On the other hand, if the conclusion you espouse is not supported by the available data, or if you refuse to consider alternative hypotheses, or fail to acknowledge subjective interpretation methods in your field, you will not demonstrate confidence and will not be believable. (Note: Insisting on projecting confidence in the face of clearly contradictory facts does not advance juror confidence in your believability.)

Ability to Persuade

Do you remember the last time you changed your mind on any subject? What caused you to do that? Did you read a book, attend a lecture, watch a television program, or exchange ideas with persons who had more information than you? As human beings, we change our minds for various reasons. One of your objectives as an expert witness may be to persuade a fact finder of the reliability of a scientific, technical, or factual proposition.

Your task is to persuade without becoming an advocate, to convince without argument, and to encourage a conclusion based upon irrefutable data presented in an interesting way. Effective persuasion is subtle. A person is most strongly convinced if he or she can mentally develop the ultimate conclusion on their own rather than it being spoon-fed by the persuader.

Enthusiasm

Enthusiasm for the task at hand, the subject matter, and the conclusion can be demonstrated in many subtle ways. Facial expression and body language tell a great deal about the witness's enthusiasm for the subject. Tone of voice and inflection can suggest boredom or conviction. If you are not interested in what you do and have done, why should the jury be?

Conclusion

A general understanding may help alleviate some of your fears of the adversary system and our dispute resolution process. If the evidence in a particular case is subject to only one conclusion and is cast in terms of absolute proof, the matter will probably not proceed to trial or hearing, unless no reasonable offer has been made for the defendant to consider. It is often the case that questionable evidence, doubtful outcomes, or conflicting testimony require adversarial presentation. That presentation and its ultimate objective, the justice process, will be aided immeasurably by your service as a forensic witness. As a reminder, justice is for the philosopher, truth is for the sage. However, it is a wise and practical society that endeavors to use the adversarial system and your expert testimony to assist the justice system.

Review Questions

1. What is the difference between a bench trial and a jury trial?
2. What is the difference between a trial court and an appellate court?
3. What could cause you to be in contempt of court? What are the consequences?
4. Which is the trier of fact: The judge or the jury? Explain.
5. Is a justice of the peace the same as a judge? Explain.
6. What is a mistrial?
7. A prosecutor works for _____ while a defense attorney works for _____.
8. Is rhetoric different from a narrative? Explain.
9. Place in the proper order, most local to most national: Small claims court, Supreme Court of the United States, U.S. Court of Appeals, U.S. District Court.
10. What is voir dire?

Discussion Questions

1. Do scientists and attorneys both engage in narratives? If so, how are they different; if not, why not?
2. When asked if it would make him nervous to use an expert who would sell his opinion for the right price, an attorney responded, "It doesn't because you know what the son-of-a-bitch will say."[10] What does this say about the professional cultures of attorneys and scientists?
3. One participant, an attorney, of the National Research Council's workshop on expert testimony said, "Science can sometimes get it wrong … Science is not always value-free, and most importantly … when lawyers accept the validity of an established scientific paradigm uncritically, they do risk making the same mistake as scientists." What do you think "the same mistakes" are? How can those mistakes be prevented or corrected?

Notes

1. Welsh, A., *Strong Representations: Narrative and Circumstantial Evidence in England* (Baltimore: Johns Hopkins University Press, 1992).
2. Evidence based on inference and not on personal knowledge or observation. Thus, all physical evidence is "circumstantial evidence," which means it is not weak or a lesser form of evidence.

3. Welsh, A., *Strong Representations: Narrative and Circumstantial Evidence in England* (Baltimore: Johns Hopkins University Press, 1992), p. 9.
4. Garfield, M., "*New Yorker* author analyzes Microsoft 'Trial of the Century,'" *Davidson News & Events*, January 22, 2001, p. 1.
5. For example, the Federal Judicial Center offers training and resources to judges at www.fjc.gov.
6. The phrase voir dire comes from the Old French for "speak the truth."
7. *New York Times*, December 28, 1879, p. 6; as quoted in Golan (2004), 164.
8. For example, thermal cooling (*Kelvin v. Darwin*), the motions of stars (*Kepler v. Greeks*), combustion (*Priestly v. Stahl*), discovery of fingerprints (*Faulds v. Henry*); note also, the conflict need not be personal, for example, the miasmatic theory of disease versus the germ theory.
9. National Research Council, *The Age of Expert Testimony: Science in the Courtroom* (Washington, DC: National Academy Press, 2002), p. 23.
10. Prichard, F., *Experts in Civil Cases: An Inside View* (New York: LFB Scholarly Publishing, LLC, 2005), p. 88.

The Legal Context

4

Key Terms

Deposition
Discovery
Exculpatory evidence
Federal Rules of Civil Procedure
Interrogatories
Privileged

Introduction

This chapter discusses some of the most important tools in the legal system's kit to ensure all parties have all and the same information. Discovery, depositions, and the Rules of Evidence (either Federal (FRE) or state specific) are not only for attorneys—the well-prepared expert would do well to review these tools and understand what will be expected of him or her. Discovery, depositions, and the Rules of Evidence are both a sword and a shield.

Discovery

Discovery has been defined as "compulsory disclosure, at a party's request, of information that relates to the litigation."[1] Discovery can involve any material that is relevant to the case except information that is privileged (protection for communications between certain parties, such as a client and his attorney, and makes them confidential) information that is the work product of the opposing party, or certain kinds of expert opinions. Under most rules of civil procedure, discovery tools include statements on oral or written questions, written interrogatories, production of tangible items, property, physical and mental examinations, and requests for admission.

In criminal cases, discovery includes material in information either in the possession of the prosecutor or in the control of the prosecutor. It may include police reports, witness statements, laboratory reports, a defendant's statement, charts, graphs, photographs, tangible objects such as items collected

DOI: 10.4324/9781003610540-4

at a crime scene, etc. How this information is obtained by the defense varies by jurisdiction. All prosecutors, however, are bound by the Brady decision of the Supreme Court of the United States. Prosecutors are bound to disclose exculpatory evidence, which is evidence that tends to negate the defendant's guilt. Withholding evidence "casts the prosecutor in the role of an architect of a proceeding that does not comport with standards of justice" (*Brady v. Maryland*, 373 U.S. 83, 88 [1963]). The facts in *Brady* involved a statement given to police that the police did not provide to the prosecution. Nonetheless, the Supreme Court held failure to disclose that evidence was a violation of the defendant's right to a fair trial. Experts, in particular, experts who work for the government, should be mindful of the prosecution's obligation to disclose evidence to the defendant. Under no circumstances should an expert fail to disclose information to the attorney they are working with. It will be up to the lawyer, not the expert, to decide whether something is, or is not, subject to discovery in any given case.

In layman's terms, discovery is the sometimes laborious process you go through to learn the underlying facts surrounding a matter in dispute. Certain devices are available by rules of procedure or practice in the various jurisdictions to help uncover underlying facts. Some lawyers think that discovery is the key to really getting to the fact basis for litigation. Others consider discovery the bane of their existence and the weight that is driving the justice system to unfathomable depths. Regardless of an attorney's point of view about the process, the exchange of discovery allows attorneys the opportunity to evaluate the strengths and weaknesses of their case. This frequently leads to case resolution prior to trial.

All procedural rules must be liberally construed to secure just, speedy, and inexpensive dispute resolution.[2] The Federal Rules of Civil Procedure (Fed. R. Civ. P.) govern civil procedure in the U.S. district courts. The Fed. R. Civ. P. are promulgated by the U.S. Supreme Court and then approved by the Congress. The federal courts use the Fed. R. Civ. P. as their rules of procedure in civil cases (where the dispute is typically over money). States, although they produce rules that apply in their own courts, have largely adopted rules that are based on the Federal Rules. In the federal system, civil discovery is governed by Fed. R. Civ. P. Title V, "Depositions and Discovery," Rules 26–37 (see Table 4.1).

Discovery and inspection in federal criminal cases are generally governed by Federal Rules of Criminal Procedure (Fed. R. Crim. P.) 15 and 16. As with the civil rules of procedure, the states have their own version of the rules of criminal procedure. While many rules mirror the Federal Rules, each state's rules may vary in one way or another from the Federal Rules.

The idea behind the rules of discovery is best stated in the rules themselves. According to Rule 26 of the Fed. R. Civ. Pro.:

Table 4.1 Title V of the Federal Rules of Civil Procedure, Rules 26–37, that govern depositions and discovery.

V. Depositions and Discovery
Rule 26. Duty to Disclose; General Provisions Governing Discovery
Rule 27. Depositions to Perpetuate Testimony
Rule 28. Persons Before Whom Depositions May Be Taken
Rule 29. Stipulations About Discovery Procedure
Rule 30. Depositions by Oral Examination
Rule 31. Depositions by Written Questions
Rule 32. Using Depositions in Court Proceedings
Rule 33. Interrogatories to Parties
Rule 34. Producing Documents, Electronically Stored Information, and Tangible Things, or Entering onto Land, for Inspection and Other Purposes
Rule 35. Physical and Mental Examinations
Rule 36. Requests for Admission
Rule 37. Failure to Make Disclosures or to Cooperate in Discovery; Sanctions

> (1) Scope in General. Unless otherwise limited by court order, the scope of discovery is as follows: Parties may obtain discovery regarding any nonprivileged matter that is relevant to any party's claim or defense and proportional to the needs of the case, considering the importance of the issues at stake in the action, the amount in controversy, the parties' relative access to relevant information, the parties' resources, the importance of the discovery in resolving the issues, and whether the burden or expense of the proposed discovery outweighs its likely benefit. Information within this scope of discovery need not be admissible in evidence to be discoverable.

The rules typically should be construed "to secure the just, speedy, and inexpensive determination of every action and proceeding."[3] Similarly, the Federal Rules of Criminal Procedure are designed "to be interpreted to provide for the just determination of every criminal proceeding, to secure simplicity in procedure and fairness in administration, and to eliminate unjustifiable expense and delay."[4]

Discovery affects experts in two distinct ways. First, experts are an important source of information to support the case. Second, an expert's work, investigation, and opinion may be the subject of discovery effort by opposing counsel.

The Discovery Components

Under the Federal Rules of civil discovery that attend most court proceedings, the following general devices make up the discovery arsenal:

- Written interrogatories, or questions to an opposing party or witness
- Verbal deposition, or the informal process of taking sworn testimony from witnesses before trial
- Requests for production of documents, tangible things, entry onto land or other property to inspect, measure, survey, photograph, test, or sample the property or object
- Physical and mental examination of parties and examination of premises
- Requests for admission, designed to eliminate issues from trial.

The rules of civil discovery differ from rules of criminal discovery. The constitutional guarantee against self-incrimination limits discovery from defendants in criminal cases. This is based on the Fifth Amendment to the Constitution, which holds that defendants in a criminal case cannot be forced to testify against themselves or give evidence against their own interest.

The Republic's founders were concerned about forced confessions, so much so that protection from self-incrimination is deeply ingrained in our criminal law practice. Because of the fear of forced self-incrimination, the prosecution in a criminal case has limited access to the files, records, documents, and projected testimony of a criminal defendant prior to trial. Certain identifying items, such as DNA profiles, hair, urine, handwriting, breath, fingerprints, footprints, or voice exemplars, have been carved out as acceptable prosecution discovery products. Search warrants issued "upon probable cause" allow law enforcement access to the files, premises, and the person of a criminal suspect or defendant.

Defendants are allowed to probe government files in preparation for trial. Both the Federal Rules of Criminal Procedure and state rules typically allow some discovery by defendants. For example, the government must disclose statements of the defendant, including, in some jurisdictions, the defendant's grand jury testimony, the defendant's prior criminal record, documents, other objects that are intended to be evidence at trial, and reports of examinations and tests, as well as a written summary of the anticipated testimony of expert witnesses. The government does not have to disclose internal government documents, inspections, or reports in connection with an investigation or prosecution of a criminal case, or statements made by government witnesses or prospective government witnesses, except as provided by detailed statutory exceptions.[5]

Under the Federal Rules of Criminal Procedure, a defendant must provide copies of documents that are intended to be used at trial, if the defendant has asked for production from the government. The same is true for reports of examinations and tests, provided the defendant intends to present that evidence at trial. Defense memos or documents created in connection with the investigation or defense of the case by the defendant, the defendant's attorney, or their agents, which include experts, need not be produced.

Under the FREs and in some states, depositions may be taken if exceptional circumstances are shown and it is in the interest of justice. In other states, depositions are taken in criminal cases as a matter of course.

The rules of the relevant jurisdiction specifies what objects the defendant may obtain under criminal procedures disclosure rules. While discovery rules vary by jurisdiction from state to state, typically, the following are subject to discovery in criminal cases:

- Arrest reports
- Investigative reports
- Statements of witnesses
- Statements of the accused (whether written or oral)
- Grand jury transcripts (in some jurisdictions)
- Tangible evidence
- Results of physical, mental, and scientific tests
- Results of experiments or comparisons
- Books, papers, documents, photographs, or other tangible things that will be evidence in the case
- Access to buildings and relevant places
- Record of prior criminal convictions of the accused or co-defendant
- Tapes and transcripts of electronic surveillance
- Electronic data

In addition, in some jurisdictions, the following materials may be produced only by court order (in other jurisdictions, no such order is required; in still other jurisdictions, some of the following is only accessible under certain specific circumstances):

- Material in possession of other governmental agencies
- Defendant's expert reports or statements
- Physical or mental examination of defendant or other witnesses
- Scientific experiments or comparisons

Almost all rules of discovery, civil and criminal, mandate a continuing duty on the part of a responding party to update responses based on additional or newly discovered information. All discovery rules, both civil and criminal, typically have sanction provisions by which the court can enforce its orders and require compliance.

The Expert and the Discovery Process

The expert's initial attitude may be:

> Well, discovery is nice for the attorneys and the litigants, but it doesn't have anything to do with me. I'm a scientist. I'll do my work and research the way I've always done it, without cumbersome rules of procedure that require continuous jumping through ever-diminishing hoops, and let the attorneys worry about discovery.

However, the rules do indeed apply to experts. Because the rules vary from jurisdiction to jurisdiction, and because the rules are subject to change, an expert should never presume to understand the rules of discovery.

It is important to distinguish the discovery process from standard professional or technical information-gathering procedures. Scientists gather information based upon an organized plan of investigation and inquiry; their use of investigative protocols and procedures, case plans, and action plans creates a process for getting their work done. The steps followed to complete the investigation and/or testing enable the facts and information upon which your expert opinion will be based to be collected in an orderly and logical way. Customary and routine testing, investigation, and consultation with others provide the needed facts.

Discovery, on the other hand, is structured and driven by the time deadlines imposed by court or procedural rules. Each item of discovery is undertaken in a set manner, with or without court intervention, by attorneys representing the parties. The discovery process is ultimately subject to supervision of the court. What discovery and standard expert investigation have in common is that, in each case, facts are gathered that ultimately will shape the expert's opinions, and hence, possibly the legal outcome.

An Example of a Criminal Case

A unique burglary ring was discovered in a suburban community. The leader of the gang was a young mother of two. The woman was a cult leader who conducted bizarre rituals in the basement of her modest home. Actively working in the burglary operation under her direction and supervision were her husband, her husband's brother, and a societal dropout who had recently joined the group.

The focal point of the ritual activity of the group was a satin-lined casket, which was the first item they had stolen. Criminal charges against them included many counts of burglary. In addition, the three adults were charged with contributing to the delinquency of the fourth member of the ring, who was a minor. According to the investigative reports, the cult leader motivated her followers by dispensing drugs and sexual favors, sometimes in group settings.

Each defendant was tried separately from the others. An investigator criminalist engaged by counsel for the brother-in-law discovered the existence of statements in the prosecution's files from other defendants. Appropriate motions were made under the rules of criminal procedure to require the prosecutor to produce the statements for examination prior to trial. The investigator also discovered that numerous items of stolen property were to be used as exhibits at the trial. Again, a motion that was made to the court required the prosecutor to allow the defense counsel to inspect the items before trial.

In addition, the client advised the investigator and counsel that all the accused persons had made statements to the investigating and arresting officers. Those statements had not been transcribed, although the investigator determined that one of the arresting officers had made extensive notes of conversations with the accused. The trial court granted a defense motion to reveal the officer's notes to defense counsel prior to trial.

On the prosecution side, a number of stolen items carried fingerprints that matched prints taken from various crime scenes. The police obtained a warrant to secure fingerprints from each defendant to compare with those on the items of stolen property and at the crime scenes. Some of the items of stolen property had been recovered from a garage some distance from the cult leader's home. Police had taken custody of items in that garage without a search warrant and without any showing of probable cause. Appropriate motions were made, and the evidence was suppressed by court order following a hearing.

An Example of a Civil Case

A number of years ago, a soldier at Fort Dix, New Jersey, became ill. His illness was tentatively diagnosed as swine flu. From that one case, never actually confirmed, the full power of the U.S. Public Health Service swung into action. The entire government was mobilized. Private contractors were authorized to manufacture millions of doses of swine flu vaccine. The government indemnified the manufacturers, because vaccine testing procedures were abrogated due to the perceived threat to the public health.

There was some evidence that the government concluded it had no place to store the vaccine. It was determined to literally "warehouse" the vaccine in the bodies of the people of the United States rather than incur the expense of physical storage. Testing procedures had not yet been completed. The press, radio, and television carried warnings of the dangers of swine flu and urged mass inoculation. The surgeon general of the United States made pleas. As a result, millions of people were inoculated.

Then epidemiologists started to note cases of a disease called Guillain-Barré syndrome (GBS), a neurological impediment that had from mild to fatal effects on its victims. Not much was known about GBS except that it affected the central nervous system and resulted in paralysis or weakness of various parts of the body. The attacks were unpredictable, and treatment was not well established. Massive amounts of physical therapy and drugs were prescribed for the sufferers; some never recovered.

The victims of GBS were correlated with persons who had received swine flu vaccines. It became obvious that the swine flu vaccine was the cause of the GBS outbreak. Tort litigation was commenced in many federal districts against the U.S. government and the vaccine manufacturers. The government admitted causal connection for a certain group of victims, and Congress passed a law making the government fully responsible for the claims and further indemnifying the drug manufacturers.

A multidistrict litigation panel of the federal court system was convened. Judge Gerhard Gesell of the U.S. District Court in Washington, DC was the supervising jurist of all swine flu vaccine cases. A claimants' committee undertook a first wave of discovery against the drug manufacturers and the government. Many experts were engaged to track the relationship between the swine flu vaccine and the onset of GBS. National forensic experts worked closely with a plaintiffs' steering committee to frame the discovery questions that were asked of the federal government and the drug manufacturers. Some discovery areas included:

- Diagnosis of swine flu
- Actual cases of swine flu
- Components of the swine flu vaccine
- Test procedures followed
- Test procedures that were known to be applicable, but which were not used
- Warehousing by inoculation of the vaccine without adequate testing

A number of physicians, primarily neurologists, engaged by victims throughout the country further guided the discovery process against both the drug manufacturers and the federal government. After extensive research into the disease process as compared with the vaccine components, they testified as to epidemiologic information, time relationship between inoculation and symptoms onset, uniform treatment procedures, morbidity, and available physical and drug therapy.

Depositions, interrogatory responses, and requests for production of documents, as generated by the attorneys and guided by experts, allowed many patients to reach significant settlements. In addition, some won substantial damages after trial.

The expert becomes involved in formal discovery in four ways: As a consultant who assists in generating questions for cross-examination, as an advisor in responding to the opposition's questions, as the person responding to written and verbal questions prior to trial, and finally, (perhaps most common) experts become involved in discovery when attorneys request evidence to support their conclusions. Not all experts will actively participate in the discovery process. Typically, where an expert is acting as a consultant for one side or the other, to assist in formal discovery in a meaningful way, the expert must be:

- Professionally and technically competent
- Knowledgeable about the real world
- Conversant with current literature, practice, and procedure
- Familiar with the facts of the case
- Has developed a working hypothesis
- Innovative in digging out information from the opposition
- Well schooled in the art of brevity
- Informed about the legal rules that govern the discovery process

Drafting written questions that the opposing party must answer fully and under oath, outlining areas of inquiry and constructing specific questions for use during deposition of the opposing witnesses or experts, guiding the attorney to a better understanding of your science, or performing an independent evaluation of the conclusions of another are all tasks the expert may be asked to conduct.

Preparing for Deposition or Trial Testimony

Getting ready for deposition is in many respects a preparation for a mini-trial: The same steps are required for both events. Deposition is sworn testimony outside of a courtroom. At trial, the sworn testimony is provided in court, before a judge and jury. Jury testimony will be addressed further in Chapter 5, however, the tips for deposition testimony are also true for trial testimony. It is helpful, in approaching the deposition or trial, to understand the opposing attorney's potential objectives. In general, these may include:

- To gather additional information
- To assess your demeanor as a witness
- To demonstrate to your client and attorney the extent of knowledge and expertise that the opposition possesses
- To attempt to impeach you
- To lock you into a position

It is valuable, if painful, to practice giving deposition on videotape. The attorney can ask some questions—both open-ended and closed questions—to allow the expert to review their demeanor during depositions. The benefit of observing physical mannerisms and methods of answering questions for purposes of self-improvement is crucial. Certainly not every case warrants videotaped deposition preparation, but for cases that do, the results of rehearsal can be dramatic.

Do not attend a deposition without substantial preparation. The following is a check-list of things to do before and during your deposition:

- Review your entire file
- Carefully check the accuracy of your final report
- Confer with the attorney
- Dress as you would for trial
- Get a good night's sleep before the deposition

There is a fundamental rule in discovery matters that you probably already know. Talking too much in discovery, revealing more than is required, waxing eloquent or acting egotistical, telling all you know about the entire subject—all can be detrimental to the case.

Some examples of good and bad answers to deposition questions will help you prepare. First, the bad answers:

Question: Please state your name for the record.
Answer: My name is Harvey Witness. I live at 1224 Main. My phone number is (707) 555-8811. My consulting company is known as Witness Consulting.

Comment: Obviously, the witness has violated a cardinal rule of deposition examination: He gave more information than was actually requested. See what that technique does for Mr. Witness later.

The witness has violated several cardinal rules of deposition examination. He did not listen to the question he was asked. He responded with much more information than he was asked to provide. And he tipped off the opposing counsel that he will likely continue to listen carelessly to questions and respond with excessive detail. This can be detrimental to an expert's client's case.

Question: Did you inspect the parking lot?
Answer: I did, and I will tell you there is no way that the parking lot complies with the Uniform Building Code, the architect's design, or the National Safety Council requirements.

Comment: The correct answer would have been "yes." Mr. Witness's answer opens up a whole series of questions about items that Mr. Witness may (or may not) have fully examined or be qualified to testify about. In his desire to be the consummate expert, Mr. Witness tries to tell all he knows. If he had not disclosed the three items on which he relied, examining counsel might never have asked about them. It might turn out that the three items do not support Mr. Witness's conclusion, and some backpedaling would then be required at trial. Further, attorneys have ethical obligations in regards to discovery. If the answer provided is not addressed in some fashion in the expert's summary of findings provided to opposing counsel, this could potentially result in a mistrial if the expert volunteers this information for the first time at trial.

Question: Mr. Witness, do you have an opinion as to what caused Mrs. Wally to fall in the parking lot?
Answer: Yes, I do. She fell because the concrete parking bumper she tripped over was not painted the required color. It was dark between the cars, she had her arms full of groceries. She followed her daughter into the parking lot and the daughter stepped over the parking bumper. Mrs. Wally failed to see the concrete bumper, tripped, and fell. There is absolutely no question in my mind that the failure of the store to paint the parking bumper yellow was the direct cause of the fall.

Comment: Here Mr. Witness has done quite a number of things wrong. First, instead of just answering the question with a simple "yes," he proceeded to explain everything he knew about the subject. Each piece of information he volunteered constitutes a trail for the skillful examiner to follow. The next thing he did wrong was to state his opinion in absolute terms. He forgot that many things were sufficient to have caused Mrs. Wally to fall in the parking lot, none of which are necessarily what the Witness examined. He also forgot that all he has to state is his opinion, based upon a probable—not an absolute—basis. Rarely are things "absolute." Consequently, the expert loses credibility by taking this position. Trying to help one side "win" by overstating the strength of the evidence could have dire consequences to the expert's future viability. He also opened up the defense tactic of "contributory or comparative negligence" by noting that his client failed to see what her daughter clearly saw.

Question: Is it possible, Mr. Witness, that you've made a mistake in your opinion?
Answer: Absolutely not. I can't imagine how you could even suggest that. I did my work. I made my measurements. I studied everything there was to study. I've been in this field for 35 years.

Comment: Mr. Witness has violated several more rules of good testimony procedure. He has gotten angry with the attorney and become defensive and argumentative. He has spoken in absolutes. In all respects, he has done no service to himself or his client.

After proper schooling and some video practice, Mr. Witness becomes a much improved witness.

Question: Mr. Witness, do you have an opinion as to why Mrs. Wally fell?
Answer: Yes.
Question: What is the basis for your opinion?
Answer: My investigation of the case.

Comment: At this point, examining counsel has a choice. The answer can either be accepted or probed further. A good examiner would probe further, asking for details about education, documents reviewed, when the scene was visited, etc., but if it is getting late and the witness seems to be in control of the examination, the attorney may move on to something else. That would be beneficial to Mr. Witness's client and his position as a testifying expert. He can tell all he knows at trial, not at deposition.

Question: Mr. Witness, in light of all the circumstances of this case and with a view toward your testimony at the time of trial, just what is it that you are saying and how do you explain your position at this time?
Answer: I don't understand your question; it is really two questions.
Question: Which part did you not understand?
Answer: If you could break the question down into separate questions, I'll try to answer each one as accurately as I can.

Comment: This shows Mr. Witness's understanding of the process of complex and compound questions. Numerous questions, some of which were vague and unclear, were built into the attorney's long and rambling question. Mr. Witness did right by politely asking the attorney to break the question down into separate parts.

Question: Mr. Witness, did you talk with anyone before coming into this deposition room today about your testimony?
Answer: Yes.
Question: Who did you talk to?
Answer: I talked to Ms. Booth, the prosecuting attorney.
Question: What did she tell you to say?
Answer: She told me to be truthful in all respects.
Question: Did you rehearse your testimony?
Answer: No, but I did prepare for today.

Comment: The attorney can make little response to this question-and-answer series. He should move on to something else. From that response, Mr. Witness has done right again and has been truthful and honest in his answer.

Question: Mr. Witness, what do you think could have been done to remedy this parking lot situation?
Answer: Are you asking for my opinion?
Question: I want to know what you think.
Answer: My opinion is that in all probability standard lighting and painting would have avoided the situation.

Comment: The attorney is trying to obtain a guess or speculation. Mr. Witness, persists in rendering his opinion. In trial, that opinion will be enhanced and embellished based on reasonable scientific and technical probability.

Question: Mr. Witness, are you absolutely certain the parking bumper was not painted yellow at the time of Mrs. Wally's fall?
Answer: I'm reasonably certain that was the situation.
Question: Isn't it possible that the paint wore off between the time of her fall and the time of your inspection?
Answer: My inspection of the scene occurred on July 15 and the incident occurred on July 8. I doubt the paint would have worn off in seven days.

Comment: The attorney is attempting to instill doubt and lock Mr. Witness into an absolute position, knowing that given the rules of human conduct, there are few absolutes. But because the witness framed the answer in terms of his investigation and reasonable probability, he avoids the trap. His documentation of the scene and his investigation support his position resolutely.

Question: Is it not true, Mr. Witness, that part of the responsibility for this fall must be squarely placed on Mrs. Wally for not having watched her step?
Answer: It's not my place to decide that issue.

Comment: Here Mr. Witness has shown his careful preparation of the case and his recognition of the legal principles involved. His field of expertise and technical examination do not extend to the ultimate weighing of comparative fault or contributory negligence. He knows that matters of claimant's contributory or comparative negligence are jury questions, not for determination by the design-and-construction expert.

Question: Is it correct that the amount of light available at the site of Mrs. Wally's fall is measured by your "guesstimate"?
Answer: No, that is not correct.
Question: Well, how is the light measured?
Answer: By use of standard test equipment that measures light intensity in terms of candlepower.

Comment: At this point, Mr. Witness is tempted to, but did not, go into techniques of measurement, description of standardization equipment, recognized scientific procedures, methods by which lighting was tested, and precautions that he took to make sure the test was done at the same time of day Mrs. Wally fell. If examining counsel wishes to go into those items, he will. If not, the matter is best left for sponsoring counsel to explore at trial.

Your deposition may be preceded by a required written report and a series of written interrogatories. Examining counsel has the right to select any reasonable means of discovery. Written interrogatories may be used; these are formal written questions that require an answer.

Some of the questions may appear almost harassing, others may seem irrelevant; some questioning will sound like a fishing expedition. All are allowable and standard operating procedure in a deposition for opposing counsel to attempt to accomplish the previously-noted objectives. There are six areas that demand the expert's attention in preparation for deposition:

- Conversations conducted to prepare you for deposition may be discoverable
- The lawyer who attends the deposition with you may not be able to instruct you as to whether you can or cannot answer questions
- What items to volunteer in your answers must be carefully reviewed with counsel

- If you have published or testified to something inconsistent with your position, be sure to discuss this with counsel in advance
- Be open and receptive to suggestions from counsel about your behavior, attitude, and posture during testimony
- Prior drafts of your reports may be required to be produced, in some jurisdictions

When you attend your deposition, your overall air of quiet confidence and control will be immediately apparent (do not confuse arrogance with confidence! Confidence stems from knowing you have proper education, training, experience, and your review of your work confirms your conclusions). When you enter, take a moment to survey the room. You may wish to select a seat that requires others in the room to shift their position. You may want to sit with your back toward the glare of outside windows.

The papers and materials you use to refresh your memory during or before testifying may be ordered produced. Of course, if you have prepared a report that has been provided to the other side, that is the best memory refresher to use. Do not hesitate to ask for a recess if you are tired, if the questions appear to be coming too fast and furiously, or if you otherwise need a break. Recall that your words are being recorded. Long pauses are not. If you only need a moment or two to collect your thoughts, take a moment to sip your water, search your file, or just sit quietly to reflect upon the question. Do not allow counsel to rush you if you need a moment. There is nothing wrong with saying, "I need a moment to consider the question."

The deposition room often, but not always, represents a full-court press. There should be no off-the-record or informal discussions with counsel. They are a trap for the unwary and inexperienced expert. When the deposition is concluded, do not ask the attorney who hired you how you did; you will learn soon enough. Remember that any discussions you have with counsel during the recess may be inquired into by the examining attorney. Your posture will tell a great deal about how you approach the task, so walk into the room standing tall. Avoid fraternizing with anyone in the room. Sit erect, maintain eye contact, and be alert.

Take some time to evaluate the method and manner of approach of the examining attorney. Is the approach aggressive and tenacious, or does he try to "nice guy" you to death? Your early analysis will be important, both for deposition and trial. The attorney might vary his style to throw you off base. Be alert to changes in demeanor. Treat everyone at the deposition politely. Jokes or flippant comments are inappropriate. Maintain your professional demeanor at all times, but do not appear cold.

You have reviewed your facts and file. You are comfortable with your subject matter. You know more about the case than anyone else in the room.

You display an air of competence and composure, no matter how you feel internally. Your demeanor should be that of a person who is familiar with the spotlight and sufficiently accustomed to it to be comfortable there. Now begins the examination: How many hours have you devoted to the project? What have you done? Who have you seen? What tests have you performed? What do they show? What did the attorney tell you about the case? Produce every communication you have had with the lawyer. What other experts have you consulted? What did they say? What texts or periodicals did you review? Which are authoritative, in your opinion? Your skillful yet precise answers will keep the examination on track. Listen to the question asked. Answer that question, and that question only. Do not volunteer additional information. Do not presume you know where the attorney is going and jump ahead to offer the answer you anticipate they may be seeking. If the lawyers want more information beyond the question immediately before you, know they will get to it eventually. The attorney will address your conclusions or opinions. "You concluded the children's milk was poisoned?" "In coming to this conclusion, did you consider the following facts …" "Are you aware of a recent study published in [insert peer reviewed journal here]? Did you consider the findings of that study when coming to your conclusion?"

During the deposition, do not look to the attorney who engaged your services for assistance. Your eyes must be focused on the examining attorney, no one else. Think about it. What will the opposition think of you as a witness if you have to keep looking to counsel for aid? The other side will know that, come the time of trial, you will not be able to stand up to the rigors of examination. Further, at trial, the attorney may either comment on your conduct to the jury, or stand between you and counsel, removing your safety net. Either strategy may be employed, once opposing counsel realizes your weakness.

At the conclusion of the deposition, gather any papers, say polite goodbyes to everyone in the deposition room, and leave. You will have ample opportunity to confer with counsel later. After doing well, the human tendency is to immediately review the successful event ("Man, I nailed that chain of custody question!"). Suppress that tendency. Doing poorly will also carry its own burden. A professional will leave the room as if he had done well. As in questioning, do not provide information that was not requested—if you leave the room looking arrogant or beaten, that may tell the opposing attorney something he or she did not know.

Request a copy of your transcript. A transcribed copy will be made available for review. Examine it to correct typographical errors, not to make substantive changes you have thought of since the deposition. Make the minimum number of corrections or changes possible, because the changes you make can become the basis of cross-examination at trial. An important "yes" when "no" was the right answer will be hammered hard on the stand. After the transcript is reviewed, your signature is required to approve the transcription as offered or with modifications. If you do not examine the transcript, then most local rules provide that the deposition may be filed without your signature, with approval being assumed. Therefore, always review the transcription for transmission or typographical errors.

Your deposition presents a challenge and an opportunity. The challenge will become less severe in direct proportion to the degree of your preparation; the opportunity is to display your ability as a witness, not to display all the knowledge you have amassed on the subject of this or any other case. Your calm, cool demeanor and confident professionalism should permeate the entire deposition experience.

Federal Rules of Evidence

The Federal Rules of Evidence (FRE) are the rules that govern the admissibility of evidence in the U.S. federal court system. Although the FREs apply only in federal courts, the states have adopted similar—or even identical—rules. Prior to the adoption of the FRE in 1975, case law (unofficial common law) formed the basis of the Rules of Evidence. The U.S. Supreme Court drafted versions of the FRE in 1969, 1971, and 1972. Congress then studied the FRE, ultimately allowing them to become federal law in 1975, with modifications by the Supreme Court. The Rules of Evidence in broad measure tend to admit evidence that is helpful, reliable, trustworthy, and assists the jury in determining whether a party has proved or disproved an issue in a case.The FRE are divided into eleven articles, with each article containing one or more rules. The articles are:

- General Provisions
- Judicial Notice
- Presumptions in Civil Actions and Proceedings
- Relevancy and Its Limits
- Privileges
- Witnesses
- Opinions and Expert Testimony
- Hearsay
- Authentication and Identification
- Contents of Writings, Recordings, and Photographs
- Miscellaneous Rules

General Rules Regarding Witness Testimony

There are over 60 FREs, many of which have multiple subsections. The purpose of the Rules of Evidence is to "administer every proceeding fairly, eliminate unjustifiable expense and delay, and promote the development of evidence law, to the end of ascertaining the truth and securing a just determination" (FRE 102; 2017). The following is a brief discussion of some of the relevant FREs, as they relate to testimony. Note, these rules may vary in form and substance at the state level. People are considered competent to be witnesses unless the Rules of Evidence or the rules of the court or statutes provide otherwise (FRE 601). Generally, witnesses may not testify unless they have personal knowledge of the matter in issue, with one major exception, and that is regarding experts who may render opinions even if they did not have personal knowledge of the facts at the time the case arose (FRE 602). Oath or affirmation is customarily given to testify truthfully. This oath is issued in a form "designed to impress that duty on the witness's conscience" (FRE 603).

The credibility of a witness may be attacked by any party, and that includes the party who called the witness in the first instance (FRE 607). Opinion and reputation evidence going to the credibility, or lack thereof, of a witness may be admitted, but only to show past character for truthfulness or untruthfulness. This evidence is only allowed if the witness has been attacked as to credibility or reputation. Specific instances of conduct of the witness supporting or attacking credibility may not be used to attack credibility, except in very narrow circumstances (FRE 608).

A witness may be impeached by proving conviction of a serious crime for which imprisonment in excess of a year is called for, however, before admission the court must perform an analysis of the probative nature of the conviction. If the witness has been pardoned or the conviction annulled, the conviction is not admissible (FRE 609). Religious beliefs of a witness are not admissible to bear on the credibility of the witness (FRE 610).

Generally, the court controls the method and order of questioning. Leading questions should generally not be used on direct examination except as foundation testimony. The contrary is true on cross-examination, where leading questions are permitted. Leading questions may also be used for hostile witnesses, an adverse party, and witnesses associated with an adverse party (FRE 611). Writings may be used to refresh the witness's memory. If used, such writing may be inspected by the adverse party (FRE 612). A witness may be examined concerning a prior statement, but that statement does not have to be shown to the witness. However, upon request, the party must disclose the statement to opposing counsel. When a party seeks to introduce extrinsic evidence of a prior inconsistent statement by a witness, the witness must have the opportunity to either explain or deny the statement (FRE 613).

A court may call witnesses on its own motion. In this circumstance, both parties are entitled to cross-examine the witness. The court may also examine or cross-examine a witness regardless of who called the witness (FRE 614).Finally, and perhaps most important, courts have the power to exclude witnesses so they cannot hear another witness's testimony. There are exceptions to this, including, under the Federal Rules, the presence of a person, such as an expert, who is essential to a party's case (FRE 615 (c)).

FREs Regarding Expert Testimony and Opinion Testimony

Generally only experts may testify as to opinions or inferences, except if lay opinion is tendered based upon the perception of a witness (for example, speed, intoxication, mental state), such testimony would be helpful to a clear understanding of the witness's testimony, and the testimony is not based on specialized knowledge, such as scientific or technical knowledge, which is governed by Rule 702 (FRE 701).

Experts may, for the most part, give opinions about the ultimate issue to be decided by the trier of fact. This opinion is not automatically objectionable simply because it goes to the ultimate issue. However, there are limits on such testimony (FRE 704).

The expert may testify in terms of opinion and give reasons therefore without first testifying to the underlying facts or data, unless the court requires otherwise. However, the underlying facts or data are still subject to cross-examination (FRE 705).

In certain cases, the court can appoint experts either on its own motion or at the request of the parties. Court-appointed experts can be called and cross-examined by either party. The compensation for expert witnesses appointed by the court is determined by the court in accordance with rules of court or local statutes. Nothing about this rule prevents either party from calling their own experts if they choose (FRE 706).

Federal Rules of Evidence 702 and 703

Experts should be most familiar with FREs 702 and 703, as they pertain directly to them. FRE 702 was revised in 2023 and a discussion of those revisions is provided below.

FRE 702

A witness who is qualified as an expert by knowledge, skill, experience, training, or education may testify in the form of an opinion or otherwise if **the proponent demonstrates to the court that it is more likely than not that**:

(a) the expert's scientific, technical, or other specialized knowledge will help the trier of fact to understand the evidence or to determine a fact in issue;
(b) the testimony is based on sufficient facts or data;
(c) the testimony is the product of reliable principles and methods; and
(d) the expert's opinion **reflects a reliable application** of the principles and methods to the facts of the case.

The bolded text in FRE 702 is the portion revised in 2023, inspired by a law review article[6] where the authors argued that, despite FRE 702 being revised in 2000 to codify doctrines in response to *Daubert v. Merrell Dow, General Electric v. Joiner*, and *Kumho Tire v. Carmichael*, a handful of federal judges were not fulfilling their gatekeeping role to keep "bad science" out of court proceedings. Basically, some judges weren't following FRE 702, which says that they should carefully examine not only the methods an expert uses, but also how they apply those methods to the specific case. The authors pointed out many court cases where judges had allowed experts to testify, even though their testimony wasn't reliable. They argued that this had led to a situation where the quality of expert testimony depended on which court heard the case, or even which judge was assigned; this was causing unequal justice in the federal courts. Scientists were also worried that some expert testimony about forensic methods wasn't based on solid evidence, like saying evidence comes from one and only one source.[7] They pointed out that courts often relied on old decisions that just assumed these methods were valid, which meant that some experts could exaggerate how accurate their conclusions were.

FRE 703

An expert may base an opinion on facts or data in the case that the expert has been made aware of or personally observed. If experts in the particular field would reasonably rely on those kinds of facts or data in forming an opinion on the subject, they need not be admissible for the opinion to be admitted. But if the facts or data would otherwise be inadmissible, the proponent of the opinion may disclose them to the jury only if their probative value in helping the jury evaluate the opinion substantially outweighs their prejudicial effect (FRE 703, 2017).

Conclusions

In FRE 702, you will notice the core of the issues visited later by the courts in Daubert, Kumho, and Joiner: What are sufficient facts or data? What does "reliable" mean? How do we know if a method is reliable? How can we tell if that method has been applied reliably in the case at hand? For the expert witness, these can be frustrating questions in that scientists will answer them one way, but the courts may answer them another. A good rule to follow is to stick to the science that supports your professional discipline and let the courts decide what they want. You will be held accountable for your science, not your knowledge of legal decisions.

Review Questions

1. What is discovery?
2. What is a privileged communication?
3. The Federal Rules of Civil Procedure govern what, are created by whom, and who approves them?
4. What is the difference between discovery in the civil and criminal courts?
5. What is a deposition?
6. What is an interrogatory?
7. Why should you request a copy of a transcript of your deposition?
8. What are the Federal Rules of Evidence, when were they adopted, and what was used before they were adopted?
9. Which Federal Rules of Evidence are the most important for the expert to know?
10. How do the Federal Rules of Evidence define an "expert"?

Discussion Questions

1. How is deposition similar to testimony in court? How should one prepare for deposition?
2. Does the definition of an expert, according to FRE 702, seem specific or vague? Why do you think it has been defined this way?
3. What is the purpose for the difference between civil and criminal discovery?

Notes

1. Garner, B.A., *Black's Law Dictionary*, 10th ed. (St. Paul, MN: West Publishing, 2014) citing, Fed. R. Civ. P. 26–37; Fed. R. Crim. P. 16.
2. Federal Rules of Civil Procedure, Rule 1(a).
3. Federal Rules of Civil Procedure, Rule 1.
4. Federal Rules of Criminal Procedure, Rule 2.
5. 18 U.S.C. 3500.
6. Bernstein, D.E. and Lasker, E.G., "Defending *Daubert*: It's Time to Amend Federal Rule of Evidence 702," William & Mary Law Review, 57 (2015), p. 1.
7. For example, see Eldridge, H., "The Shifting Landscape of Latent Print Testimony: An American Perspective." *Journal of Forensic Science and Medicine*, 3, no. 2 (2017), pp. 72–81; Koen, W.J. and Bowers, C.M., eds., *Forensic Science Reform: Protecting the Innocent* (Academic Press, 2016).

5 Testimony

Key Term

Jury education

Introduction

Arguably, testimony is the most important thing a forensic scientist does, second only to the quality of his or her work. Testimony is also unique. Think of various situations where spoken communication is important, such as conversations, lectures, plays and movies, speeches, and songs. Testimony is, unlike any of these forms of spoken communication:

- Highly structured
- Interactive, but mostly on someone else's terms
- Narrowly focused
- Of indeterminate length
- Directed by someone else's agenda
- Limited in scope based on Rules of Evidence, Procedure, case law, constitutional protections, and pretrial rulings

Routine testimony is also unique to forensic scientists: No other scientific discipline is required to testify as a part of their job.

Some attorneys, in an attempt to either calm or throw off a witness, will say, "We're just going to have a little conversation, here …" The wise expert will ignore this oversimplification and stay attentive because nothing could be further from the truth. Expert testimony does seem simple at the outset—answer the questions and tell the truth. It is not, however, that simple. Rather, testimony may be one of the most difficult forms of spoken communication humans conduct, for a number of reasons. First, expert testimony requires a simplification of very technical information to an audience who does not necessarily have any knowledge of the topic. This "translation" is targeted at

DOI: 10.4324/9781003610540-5

a specific concept or concepts in a particular case. However, the concept and case are actually larger and editing is necessary.

> The lawyer and the expert must come to understand that they will always feel a need to say more about a technical concept that is being translated by the expert for the fact finder. But this is the impossible goal of a perfect translation, and in the courtroom there is practically never enough time to realize this dream. It is crucial that the expert and the lawyer come to agreement about what amount of testimony is enough to make clear the meaning that must be communicated … A successful presentation allows the fact finders to trust in the expertise of the witness and to apply his translation of the scientific and technical concepts and findings to the issues that the fact finders must decide.[1]

Second, the rules governing testimony are layered and intricate, spanning English grammar and vocabulary through scientific methodology and into federal, state, or local laws, and even "house rules" of particular judges or jurisdictions. Finally, the question-and-answer format is almost always done in an adversarial setting. In addition to rules regarding the form and nature of questions, opposing counsel is entitled to object if they feel the question, the answer, or the potential answer is somehow beyond the limits of what is appropriate. A simple conversation? Hardly.

This chapter covers some basics on testimony itself. The two main forms of testimony, direct and cross, will be handled in separate chapters.

Your Report

Although testimony is verbal, it starts with written words: Your report. Your report should demonstrate organization, clarity, neatness, and completeness. Its contents will depend on the scope of your analysis and form the basis for your testimony. The following recommended list of items for inclusion is intended to suggest possible areas to consider:

- The name, business address, and official title of the expert
- Contact information for the examiner or relevant contact person depending on lab policy
- The name and address of the expert's agency or business affiliation
- The date the report was issued
- The case identification information (laboratory number, case number, etc.)
- General description of the items examined

- The methods and instrumentation used to examine and analyze the submitted items
- The results of the examinations and analysis
- Any interpretations or statistics that are relevant to the results
- A statement of the disposition of the evidence
- The signatures of the examiner and any reviewers of the report
- The limits of the science
- Measurement uncertainty (where applicable)

The format of the report should roughly follow that of a standard scientific paper: Introduction, Materials and Methods, Results, Conclusions, and Discussion. You will find that most laboratory reports do not, however, have this structure. The reports may read as simply as:

> Item 1 was found to contain cocaine, a controlled substance. The net weight was 5.24 grams.

This terse approach to writing forensic reports does not tell the reader much. Unlike a scientific paper in a peer-reviewed journal, a forensic science laboratory report is not primarily intended for other scientists—most of the readers of a forensic science laboratory report are law enforcement officers, attorneys, and judges, all of whom may have little to no training in science. This lack of training requires a special effort to make the reports readable, intelligible, and concise. Many laboratories have traded completeness and documentation of procedures for a protective style: If a scientist does not tell how he analyzed something, perhaps no questions will be asked. Forensic science laboratory reports should be summations of analyses, but should also be transparent as to methods, instrumentation, and results.

The DNA revolution in forensic science led to a very different style of report writing for the biological forensic sciences:

> Item 1
>
> Human DNA was isolated from the swabbings of the waistband (Item B). The DNA obtained from the swabbings of the waistband (Item B) was amplified with the polymerase chain reaction (PCR) method and typed for twenty STR genetic markers and amelogenin, a gender-specific genetic marker, using the [lab appropriate] amplification kit.
>
> An STR DNA profile that is a mixture of DNA from at least two individuals was detected from the swabbings of the waistband (Item B). This mixture includes at least one male contributor.

This language may be followed by language such as:

- Assuming DNA from only two individuals in this mixture, a major female contributor can be determined at X number of genetic markers. Female suspect A is the source of the major female DNA from this Item.
- A major profile can be determined. Female suspect A cannot be excluded as a possible contributor of DNA from this Item.
- The minor STR data obtained is suitable for exclusionary purposes only due to the limited amount of statistical information available. Based on the STR DNA types detected, the possible contribution of DNA from the male suspect is inconclusive.
- The minor STR data obtained is suitable for exclusionary purposes only due to the limited amount of statistical information available. Based on the STR DNA types detected, the male suspect is excluded.
- The sample was amplified and typed at D1S1656, D2S441, D2S1338, TPOX, D3S1358, FGA, D5S818, CSF1PO, D7S820, D8S1179, D10S1248, THO1, vWA, D12S391, D13S317, D16S539, D18S51, D19S433, D21S11, and D22S1045.

Item 2

Human DNA was isolated from the swabbing of the hat (Item A). The DNA obtained from the swabbing of the hat (Item A) was amplified with the polymerase chain reaction (PCR) method and typed for twenty STR genetic markers and amelogenin, a gender-specific genetic marker, using the [lab appropriate] amplification kit.

A single source STR DNA profile was detected from the swabbing of the hat (Item A). Statistical calculations were performed using population statistics from databases of unrelated African American, Caucasian, and Hispanic individuals.

The probability of randomly selecting an unrelated individual with a matching DNA profile D1S1656, D2S441, D2S1338, TPOX, D3S1358, FGA, D5S818, CSF1PO, D7S820, D8S1179, D10S1248, THO1, vWA, D12S391, D13S317, D16S539, D18S51, D19S433, D21S11, and D22S1045 as obtained on the hat swab (Item A) is approximately:

- 1 in 310 sextillion in the Caucasian population
- 1 in 38 septillion in the Black population
- 1 in 83 sextillion in the Hispanic population

Although the jargon could be cleared up a bit and the prose made more readable, this is the way more forensic reports should look. In preparing your report, use internal quality assurance and final check procedures. Recheck all calculations; make sure technical terms are used correctly. Review the report for typographical errors, grammar and syntax, and clarity. The sequence of pages, exhibits, and attachments should be verified. Finally, make sure your report is distributed only to the proper recipients. All too often, experts rely on technical and administrative review to "catch" errors before a report leaves the laboratory. Experts should be mindful any errors in the work product will forever be attributable to them and them alone, regardless of who was supposed to provide a second read.

Preparation for Testimony and Communicating with Attorneys

The title of this section may suggest an oxymoron, in that some think it is impossible to communicate with attorneys. It's no shocker that lawyers and scientists often struggle to communicate in court. The fields of law and science are about as different as they can be. Law focuses on past events and relies on precedent, while science looks to the future, always searching for new truths. Additionally, scientific propositions are tested through repeatable experiments, whereas legal theories stem from unique past events that can't be replicated. Another key difference is that scientists understand that "truth" can change over time, but the legal system demands a quick resolution, so "truth" is fixed for the purpose of settling the dispute. Finally, scientists are often uneasy in court, especially during cross-examination where they must answer questions posed by lawyers and the judge. While scientific disputes are resolved gradually through peer review, legal battles are settled through cross-examination, as courts aren't meant to decide if scientific findings are right or wrong.[2] Experts have isolated problems in communicating with attorneys:[3]

- Lawyers are too busy to discuss the case
- They do not know technical language
- They do not listen to experts
- They are too aggressive and adversarial
- It is hard to get them to return phone calls
- They oversimplify complex issues
- They require yes or no answers
- They contact the expert at the last minute

Experts also suggest the following ways in which attorneys could improve the situation:

- Give the expert more time
- Plan and organize better
- Make an effort to learn the fundamentals, through reading, seminars, meetings with scientists. Recognize competence includes understanding science

Notably, lawyers also identify common communication problems:

- Scientists spend too much time attempting to explain minutiae that has little to do with the case
- Scientists use words and phrases that are too technical for lawyers to understand in a short amount of time
- Lawyers do not understand science, and scientists do not make it easy for them to do so
- Lawyers only want to focus on the area of testing they believe is relevant, and scientists frequently want to discuss other things, not relevant to the lawyer's theory of the case

Nevertheless, communication with the attorney who engaged your services, with opposing counsel, and with judges and administrative hearing officers is critical to the success of any expert witness. One of the fundamental difficulties in communicating with attorneys involves the fact that they sometimes use language differently than scientists. Further, just as scientists use some words differently than the majority of the population, so, too, do lawyers. Contrary to popular belief, legal language is not used to delay, deceive, or confuse—words are used to the specific limit of their intended resolution. A simple example may suffice. In an investigation, a person who seems to be culpable for the crime in question will be referred to as a suspect; in the courtroom, however, that person is almost always the defendant. His or her status has changed and that must be reflected in the words used to describe it. Sometimes, however, the original, not charged suspect may be referred to in court as the "third party perpetrator," if another person was subsequently charged with the crime and the defense theory is the original suspect committed the offense. As in any profession, particular terms have specific meaning; a little understanding will help the translation.

Communication between you and the attorney carries dual responsibility. You must translate technical terms and concepts for the attorney. The attorney must translate the legal vocabulary for you. A clear understanding of objectives and goals given to you by counsel will sharpen your focus. Development of one or more working hypotheses will enhance mutual understanding. To improve communication, you and the lawyer must focus together on what is to be accomplished. Opposing attorneys may try to suggest that you have been told what to say by the attorney who called you, that you have been "coached." This is why ground rules are important (see Chapter 3). You must not compromise your scientific integrity to satisfy an attorney. Having previously had a discussion on that subject allows you to testify truthfully about it, if your integrity is challenged. Discussing the case ahead of time only makes sense, and it is easy to counter the implication of bias:

Q: Did he go over with you the questions he was going to ask you by the time you took that chair to testify?
A: We reviewed the matters that I would be testifying on, yes.
Q: He told you the questions he was going to ask you, didn't he?
A: I didn't know the specific wording; I knew generally what he was going to ask, yes.
Q: And you told him what your answers would be, didn't you?
A: That's normal to review in a pretrial; yes, sir.
Q: You told him the answers, didn't you?
A: That's what I stated; yes.[4]

Do not let an attorney make a simple, sensible process like pretrial conference sound like a conspiracy. One of the easiest ways to avoid this, for those working in government labs, is for the lab policy to include meeting with any and all attorneys who ask for such a meeting. Most technical, professional, and scientific fields boast a text or series of books that constitute the core knowledge for that field. Experienced trial lawyers will regularly ask you for such texts. Failing that request, take the initiative and make that material available to the attorney. The attorney should make available to you enough information about the judicial process and your role in it for you to function effectively.

The main points during a case about which you could communicate with the attorney are:

- Understanding the overall case
- Getting to know each other's literature and vocabulary
- Drafting of interrogatories, requests for production, and deposition questions
- Preparation for deposition, both yours and the opposition
- Issuance of a final report
- Preparation for trial
- Development of direct examination questions
- Assistance in preparation of cross-examination
- Creation of exhibits

- Trial testimony
- Other trial assistance

At each of these points, confirm with counsel your understanding of what is being said to you, either verbally or in writing. Ask counsel to do the same for you. Repeating communications is an excellent way to ensure accurate understanding. Before trial, you may assist in preparing exhibits and demonstrative charts, tests, and documents. Any demonstration must be tested before the trial or hearing. The lawyers generally must show trial exhibits to opposing counsel in advance of trial. Where the parties disagree as to the relevance or admissibility of an exhibit, the court typically makes a determination well in advance of trial. Consequently, "surprise exhibits" shouldn't be created by the expert and only shown to the lawyers on the day of testimony. These are easy ways to guarantee the admissibility of a key chart, exhibit, document, or demonstration. It is proper for you to ask the attorney calling you if these details have been satisfied. Nothing can be as disappointing as preparing costly demonstrations or exhibits that are rejected at trial because of inaccuracy or lack of foundation or lack of notice. Exhibits and demonstrations must be accurate and technically correct. Demonstrations must be substantially similar to the subject under litigation to be admissible.

Preparation for trial is somewhat different from preparation for deposition. The attorney should explain to you the objectives of testimony and describe the physical setting of the hearing room in detail, including positioning of the parties, and the attorneys. The attorney should tell the expert where to position themselves in court. Entering the courtroom during another witness' testimony can have dire consequences. The attorney should outline the functions of the witnesses, attorneys, jury, or other fact finder.

Preparation for Testimony Without Communicating

There are a number of steps to follow if you are heading for trial or hearing without an opportunity to confer with counsel. Beginning these steps presupposes that you have done everything right to that point.

Consider how you will present your topic and report. Usually, identifying questions will come first, such as who you are, your relevant background, training and experience, what your assignment was, what you did, and how you did it. Your observations and tests will come next, and finally, your opinions and reasoning. Other lawyers prefer a method on direct exam referred to as "front-loading." This method asks for the expert's opinion up front. The lawyer then asks questions about your observations, your tests, and your reasoning behind your opinion. Decide when and how you will use easily understood examples to illustrate your testimony for maximum effectiveness. Because you have not spoken with the attorney, do not plan to rely on visual aids or models to illustrate your testimony. It is unlikely these will be admissible. If you cannot tell your results in three brief sentences, you do not know your material. Spend time encapsulating your analysis, findings, conclusions, and opinions into three brief statements. Practice delivering those three statements to neighbors, friends, and family members. Do they understand? Don't just presume they understand. Ask them to repeat the concepts back to you. If they cannot articulate your results, refine further.

Become familiar with the trial setting. If possible, visit the place where your testimony will be taken. Locate the witness chair and your path to it. In particular, determine the location of electric outlets and walls or screens for projection. Determine how any visual aids or exhibits may be projected. Test all of your equipment thoroughly before you use it in trial.

You should have been provided with copies of interrogatories you helped answer or draft. Review them prior to trial. Review tests, examinations, and pretrial preparations that were the subject of formal discovery response. Take particular time with the transcript of your deposition and those of concurring and contravening experts, if available. Study all these documents for strong and weak points. This will help you anticipate cross-examination.

Because you are not the lawyer, you will have no control over the order of the questions presented to you. You will only have control over how you present the evidence in response to questioning. Whether or not you appear well organized on the witness stand will tell the trier of fact a great deal about your confidence, competence, and credibility.

Leave nothing to chance. Practice, practice, practice.

You need to know when you will testify. Trials and hearings are sometimes delayed by sickness, unavailability of witnesses, or emergencies. If the attorney has not informed you of whether and when you will testify, make every attempt to contact them for guidance.

Demeanor, Dress, and Deportment

When you testify, you represent more than yourself. You are representing your laboratory, your government, and your profession. In this instance, less is more. Although it pertains to a con artist addressing his victim (a "mark"), the following advice from the 2001 movie *Ocean's Eleven* is still valuable for the expert witness on the stand.

RUSTY: How are you going to stand?
LINUS: [Hands clasped in front of him]
RUSTY: No good. And don't touch your tie. Look at me. OK. I ask you a question and you have to think of the answer, where do you look?
LINUS: [Looks down]
RUSTY: No good. You look down, they know you're lying. [LINUS looks up] And up, they know you don't know the truth. Don't use seven words when four will do. Don't shift your weight. Look always at your mark but don't stare. Be specific but not memorable. Be funny but don't make him laugh. He's got to like you and then forget you the moment you've left his sight. And for God's sake, whatever you do, don't, under any circumstances–
[Off screen]: Russ!
RUSTY: Yeah?
[Off screen]: Can you take a look at this?
RUSTY: Sure [walks off].

Whatever the unspoken advice Rusty intended to give Linus, the previous statements are all valuable to remember. The good expert witness knows that they are the conduit for the information the court needs to hear. The trial and testimony is not about them, *per se*, but about the evidence, how it was handled and analyzed, and what it means.

Even if you do not care how you look personally, all those whom you are representing do. You owe it to them, at least, to look presentable and professional. Further, courts frequently have dress codes for professionals. You should dress like you are at a job interview. You can express your "special" personal style after work and on the weekends. Dressing properly for court is easy and does not have to be expensive. Court is not the time to express yourself through your wardrobe. The center of attention is the evidence, not you. The basics are easy and apply equally to men and women:

- Black, navy, or gray suit (matching jacket and slacks/skirt) that is solid color or pinstriped
- White or blue shirt/blouse
- Black shoes (and belt for men)—polish them
- Clean, trimmed fingernails
- Empty pockets—no jingling change or bulges
- No gum, candy, or cigarettes
- Briefcase or portfolio
- Less is more. Keep your look simple

A few other specific do's and don'ts:

- Men
    - Silk necktie with an unobtrusive pattern (no clip-ons)
    - Neat, clean, trimmed head hair; avoid facial hair
    - Wedding ring and college ring only
    - No earrings or other visible body piercings
    - Cover tattoos
    - Dress shirts do not have short sleeves
    - Socks should be a shade darker than your suit
    - Full-length overcoats should be worn in winter
    - Avoid cologne
- Women
    - Always wear a suit—no dresses
    - No stilettos or boots; flats or modest heels only
    - Hosiery at or near skin color
    - No more than one ring per hand
    - Your hair should be neat and out of your face
    - One pair of earrings only; remove other visible piercings
    - Cover tattoos
    - Skirts should hang at least to the knee
    - Skirts should be straight, not pleated or gathered
    - Cleavage has no place in the courtroom
    - Carry only a briefcase to the witness stand; no purses
    - Other than noted, no additional jewelry
    - Avoid perfumes

This may seem overly conservative, and that is the point: Court is a serious event and the impression you give the jury will reflect the nature of your work—serious and professional. Someone's livelihood or life is at stake. You are testifying both by your words and your demeanor. Dress the part.

At Trial

At trial your testimony will be divided into three phases and four main parts:

- Phase 1
    - Your qualifications as an expert to render opinion testimony (voir dire)

- Phase 2
    - Direct examination
    - Your work and how it was performed
    - Findings of fact based on your analysis
    - Your expert opinions and interpretations
    - The reasons that support your conclusions
- Phase 3:
    - Cross-examination concerning facts in evidence, your direct examination, your file, your conclusions, your laboratory, and/or your science

Your qualifications are based on your education, training, and experience. A series of typical questions is offered below; it may and should be altered as your career advances.

- Please state your name
- How are you employed?
- Where did you work prior to your current position?
- What is your educational background?
- Are you a member of any professional organizations?
- Do you have any publications?
- Have you received any specialized training in your field?
- Have you taken any competency tests?
- Have you taken any proficiency tests?
- What is the nature of your work? What are you authorized to do?
- Why are these types of examinations or analyses conducted?

At this point, the sponsoring attorney may ask the court that you be qualified as an expert in a specific type of examination or discipline. The opposing attorney may want to question you regarding your qualifications in an attempt to discredit or even disqualify you, lay foundations for questions to be posed later, or just "rattle your cage." Alternately, the opposing attorney may stipulate to your qualifications; he may prefer the jury not hear how much of an expert you are. It is also possible the opposing attorney may stipulate to your qualifications because they simply do not care about your testimony. Remember, it is always possible that the opposing counsel doesn't find your testimony relevant to their theory of the case. Don't take this personally. For example, if a defendant is claiming self defense, the defendant won't care whether or not you have matched his fingerprints to the weapon or the victim's DNA to the defendant's clothing. These are points that the prosecution may feel compelled to put into evidence, but the defense may have already acknowledged this evidence.

If the judge determines that you have sufficient qualifications for what you are about to testify to, he will accept you as an expert in that particular area. Listen closely to his decision, as it will be the boundary for your expertise in this case. Being qualified as a textile fiber analyst does not necessarily mean you are qualified to testify about fabric damage. Once qualified, your direct examination begins, typically with jury education, the instruction of the jury in the necessary technical and scientific concepts and details to understand the expert's testimony sufficiently to aid in deliberation. A word about boredom. At some point in your career, you may cease to find the polymerase chain reaction as fascinating as you once did. However, when you are testifying, it is your job to present this evidence (if asked) to the jury in a compelling way. Just because it is boring to you doesn't mean it is boring to the jury. They are likely hearing this for the first time.

Your opinions may be based on facts found, tests conducted, or a series of hypothetical questions based on facts, evidence, and proof developed at trial. During the trial, you should be aware of the importance of careful testimony, particularly the hazard of inconsistent testimony between deposition and trial. You are admonished to tell the truth and to prepare for deposition or trial testimony by reviewing the facts of the case and your work effort. You should not lose your temper. Speak slowly, clearly, and naturally. If you are familiar with the process, you will not fear the examining attorney or the setting as much. You must answer only the questions asked, never volunteering information beyond the scope of the question presented. Remember that most questions asked by the other side can be answered "Yes," "No," "I don't know," "I don't remember," "I don't understand the question," or by a simple factual answer. You should not memorize your story or testimony. Avoid such phrases as "I think," "I guess," "I feel," "I believe," or "I assume." These are weak and insufficient to meet scientific and technical burdens of proof of reasonable probability.

Taking a breath—slow inhale, relaxed exhale—before answering a question is always a good idea. Taking a sip of water can also slow the pace and give you a chance to consider your answer. Let the attorney finish the question, allow a beat, then answer. Don't get anxious and jump in before the question is finished:

Attorney: Do you agree with me that the quoted text I just read to you—
Expert: Yes!
Attorney: —is inaccurate?
Expert: Uhm …

Pausing allows you to appear deliberate and gives you time to digest the question and frame an answer. Be careful of trap words such as absolutely or positively; be cautious about estimating time, space, and distance. If technical information is involved, give specifics—not estimates—in the answer. Refer to files or notes to refresh your recollection.

Avoid fencing, arguing with, or second-guessing examining counsel. If testimony could be reduced to two words, they would be patience and awareness. Patience helps you to remain calm and not rise to perceived suggestions or snarky comments from an attorney. To fence, hedge, argue, equivocate, or become angry only exposes you to further cross-examination and a resultant loss of credibility. It also draws attention to the weakness. One way to handle the situation is to answer the question and then add: "But please let me explain." The examining attorney will probably not let you do that. But the attorney for whom you are working may ask you to explain on redirect examination if they think it is important. You should not deny having had prior discussions about testimony in the case if such is the fact. If you make a mistake, correct it as soon as possible. If a negative or apparently damaging fact or omission has been elicited, admit it and move on quickly.

You should never answer too quickly or look to counsel for assistance. Testimony in court, deposition, or hearing should never be turned into a joke. Exaggeration, underestimation, or overestimation are all indications of unwary, ill-prepared, or overly confident witnesses. Translate technical terms into common, understandable language at every opportunity. Your demeanor and behavior before, during, and after testimony should be the subject of care. You should know the hazards of discussing testimony in hallways, restrooms, or public areas around the hearing room. Conversations with opposing parties, attorneys, and jurors must be avoided.

Review Questions

1. What is the most important aspect of a forensic scientist's work?
2. How is testimony different from other forms of spoken communication?
3. Testimony is based upon what?
4. How are forensic laboratory reports similar to journal research papers? How are they different?
5. Is it possible to testify without having consulted with the attorney calling you?
6. What are the three main phases of testimony?

7. What should the expert always do before answering a question during testimony?
8. If you make a mistake or misstatement on the witness stand, what should you do?
9. Should you express your personal style on the witness stand?

Discussion Questions

1. What is so important about dressing conservatively in court?
2. Why should you know what the courtroom looks like before you testify—why should that matter?
3. Go through the points you would discuss with an attorney about a hypothetical case; what must you make sure he knows? What can you disregard safely?

Notes

1. Smith, F. and Bace, R., *A Guide to Forensic Testimony* (Boston: Pearson Education, Inc., 2003), pp. 108–109. Also see Epstein, J., "The Testifying Forensic Discipline Expert—A Primer," *Wiley Interdisciplinary Reviews: Forensic Science*, 1, no. 1 (2019), p. e1320.
2. National Research Council, Policy, Global Affairs and Law Panel, *The Age of Expert Testimony: Science in the Courtroom: Report of a Workshop* (Washington, DC: National Academies Press, 2002).
3. Prichard, F., *Experts in Civil Cases: An Inside View* (New York: LFB Scholarly Publishing, LLC, 2005).
4. Bodziak, W. (testimony). *Fred Goldman et al. v. O. J. Simpson*, 43 Cal. 4th 553 (2008). November 27.

Direct Examination of Experts

6

Key Terms

ADDIE model
Bailiff
Best evidence rule
Compound question
Credibility
Direct examination
Hearsay
Hostile witness
Leading question
Objection
Recollection refreshed
Past recollection recorded
Redirect examination
TOM I PASTA

Introduction

The primary objective of effective expert testimony is to present yourself as a well-organized, informative, and credible person. The fact finders need not become amateur experts because of your testimony. They only need to be convinced you are a believable person with something important to say, who will materially assist them in doing the job of deciding the case. Whether the case is decided in support of your position is not the true measure of the effectiveness of your testimony; the true test of testimonial excellence is whether you were credible. One of the best opportunities you have to establish that trait is through direct examination. Lawyers have a saying about trials, "You are responsible for the effort—not the result." Scientists would do well to embrace this mantra. You are judged not by the verdict of "guilty" or "not guilty," but rather by your testimony, your approach to testing, your documentation in your file, your preparation, and your demeanor.

Credibility is the believability of a statement, action, or source, and the propensity of the observer to believe that statement made by the expert.

 DOI: 10.4324/9781003610540-6

In public speaking, Aristotle considered the credibility of the speaker, in essence his character, to be one of the forms of proof. Social science research and psychologists have generally found that there are multiple dimensions of credibility, but three key aspects are competence, trustworthiness, and dynamism.

You must be professionally competent and have done a thorough job of analysis, investigation, and reporting. Your individual style and demeanor must be developed. The jury must be able to trust you and your work—do not assume they will trust just because you are an expert. You should display enthusiasm without advocating. Pattern yourself after your best teachers and be prepared to illustrate your testimony graphically or with demonstrations. Prior to actually testifying, mentally visualize your best possible performance as a witness. Use of the word performance is intentional, because in a way you are performing a key role in a real-life drama. Younger experts, in particular, are cautioned. Do not take the stand as your favorite television forensic scientist or your personal forensic scientist hero. Take the stand as you. Emulate the skill set—not the character—of those you most admire. Your credibility will be established by effective use of teaching skills. Testimony is not a game, but gamesmanship is involved. A key to good testimony is to stay within your expertise, as in this example from the cross-examination of a forensic pathologist:[1]

Q	(by the defense attorney): Okay. And you would agree that's blood, correct?
A:	I would agree that that looks like blood, yes.
Q:	All right. And for a person to have bled in that particular manner, the person has to be above it, correct? Bled down on that horizontal bar, true?
Opposing Counsel:	Objection. Lack of foundation, Your Honor.
	The Court: Overruled.
	The Witness: I—
Q	(by Mr. Baker): You can answer.
A:	It looks to me—
Q:	Can you answer my question? I didn't ask—
Opposing Counsel:	If the Court please—
Q:	(by defense attorney): I didn't ask what it looks like to you.
A:	I'm not a blood spatter expert.
Q:	Would you agree that the person who left the blood there had to be above the area where the blood is dropped on the horizontal rail of the fence and then puddles into the dirt area?

Mr. Medvene: Objection. Asked and answered. The witness said he's not a blood spatter expert and he wasn't put on for that purpose.

The Court: You can answer yes or no. He testified in direct examination with regards to blood flow.

The Witness: The origin of this blood could be from a higher level. It could be from the same level.

Notice that the pathologist, although not an expert in bloodstain pattern analysis ("blood spatter") can testify about general blood flow; it was determined to be within his expertise on direct and it was allowed previously. Understanding the rules of law is critical in this situation. Experts are advised, anywhere you are willing to go on direct, you will be legally compelled to revisit, if asked on cross-examination. You are not allowed to pontificate or opine for one side, and then, when the other side inquires, claim you are not qualified to comment.

The same witness testifies at a different point in the trial:

A: My opinion of this is that it supports my conclusion that there is a single assailant with a single weapon.

Q: Well—

A: Because if there is a transfer, then there are others, of course. There is blood of one victim on the weapon, and then there will be blood on the same weapon from the next victim.

Q: Doctor, you, if that were true, there would be minuscule—that is, a small amount of—blood transferred because it would only be blood transferred by the knife, correct?

A: I cannot discuss that. I am not an expert in blood spatter. I have no expertise. I have no training. I have not read about it and I think that if I'm going to go into the detail of how much is enough, I will be misleading you and the jury and the judge.

Note the witness clearly and firmly sets the boundary.

There are several ways to present and enhance all of these factors, including positive and open body language, emphasis of key points, establishing the main points early, summarizing the main points at the conclusion of your testimony, and recognizing the need for common sense explanations.

Direct Examination and Strong Narratives

Direct examination (also called "examination in chief") is the questioning of a witness by the attorney who called her in a court of law. Direct examination is offered to provide evidence in support of facts that will satisfy or refute one or more required elements of the attorney's case. Much of direct testimony lays the foundation for what is to come or establishes facts for other witnesses; to that end, it may not be very exciting:

Q: And it was in or from that general area that you obtained these known fiber samples from the carpet?
A: It would have been underneath there, yes.
Q: Did you label and appropriately package and preserve those items?
A: Yes, I did.
Q: What item number did you give them?
A: Item no. 25.
Q: How do you recognize this item?
A: By the laboratory number, markings, and my initials on the sealed evidence tape.
Q: Did you collect other evidence while you were at that house at that particular day and time?
A: Yes, I did.
Q: Do you recognize Item no. 26?
A: Yes.
Q: How do you recognize this item?

And on and on. The basis of direct examination is what Andrew Welsch calls a strong representation.[2] Strong representations or strong narratives are factual, carefully managed narratives based upon evidence that endeavors to prove something more encompassing than personal, direct examination. First-person accounts can vary, especially in emotionally charged events.[3] As science expanded, and the faith the public had in it, physical evidence overshadowed eyewitness testimony.

Because the criminal event at issue resides in the past, the narrative is supported by the residual evidence of those events—what has been termed "proxy data." This is the essence of circumstantial evidence, the evidence of things not seen. The strong narrative is devoted to the truth, but is carefully crafted with words subtly put together (such as the difference between the vague "The hairs matched" and the more exact "The questioned hair exhibited the same microscopic characteristics as the known hairs and therefore could have originated from the same person"). Facts, however, do not explain anything by themselves. If you know the temperature outside is 82°, that alone explains nothing. Are you in Augusta, Maine or Augusta, Georgia? Is it August or April? Is that Fahrenheit or Celsius? Ultimately, facts must be subordinated to the conclusion. The expert's conclusion and the significance of the evidence are more important to the trier of fact than any one fact.

Finally, a strong narrative must purport to be true and conclusive, but only to the extent that it is capable of being so. Each inference in the narrative supposes a possible sequence of events, but not necessarily each one the right one. However, the more exhaustive the procedure for ruling out wrong inferences, the stronger the sequence of cause and effect will appear. The conclusion drawn cannot be ruled out.

Important Points to Remember

The essence of trial competence centers around projecting an image of credibility from beginning to end. Accuracy of citation, precision in factual presentation, articulate organization of graphic materials, and an organized presentation of testimony and documentary evidence are all required. As part of that credibility effort, you must project an ambiance of honesty, integrity, and believability. Given the fact both sides in a dispute tend to present often competing views of the same evidence, you must stand forth as a beacon of believability. Additional traits that are beneficial to an expert witness include being honest, open minded, well mannered, fair, polite, dynamic, and positive. You must be a good listener and project yourself as a reliable source of information. You must also testify as to the limits of science. You must admit readily when you failed to consider something, when asked. If new information changes your conclusion, or a new hypothetical could change your hypothetical conclusion, you must be willing to readily admit this.

One national authority on the subject of forensic engineering, Marvin M. Specter, founding president of the National Academy of Forensic Engineers, suggests how these factors, traits, characteristics, and techniques can be projected in the testimonial process, initially displayable on direct examination.

- Convey the fact that you are a professional, dedicated to accurate and detailed work
- Avoid any impression that you are a "hired gun" by not being drawn into biased or exaggerated statements
- Emphasize the specialized task you performed in the case, and that your testimony represents professional work and careful analysis
- Be ready to bolster your opinion with recognized technical publications
- Do not be afraid to expose the weakness of your case to counsel
- Remember that the courtroom is a serious place; your task is of utmost significance, as someone's liberty is at stake

Some points only experience teaches. They are enumerated here to highlight mistakes and observations of experienced expert witnesses and trial attorneys. Knowing about these seemingly minor admonitions will further serve your goal of increased credibility during direct examination. A descriptive vignette will illustrate salient suggestions.

As you walk in, display common courtesy to all with whom you come in contact. You never know who is a juror, hearing officer, attorney, or judge. Discuss who you are but certainly not why you are present with persons you do not know. Contact with opposing experts, regardless of your degree of friendship with them, should be minimal; a casual greeting will suffice. Potential fact finders observe hallway demeanor.

Depending on the jurisdiction and the judge's preference, the bailiff,[4] the lawyer offering the witness, or the court clerk calls the name of the witness. How you carry yourself transmits subtle messages to the audience, so walk with eyes forward, upright posture, and a confident stride. Make sure your voice, on the occasion of your first "I do," when asked if you will tell the truth, comes across loud and clear. Use your voice tone, volume, and modulation to maintain interest, vary the presentation, and keep everyone awake. Conversational normalcy is the order of the day, but make sure you can be heard clearly throughout the room. Your illustrative drawings and charts should stand alone and be self-explanatory. If called on to draw or write on a board or chart, keep your handwriting legible; and as a good performer, never turn your back on the audience. When testifying about a chart, photo, map, or other visual aid, recall a court reporter is taking down your testimony. The purpose of this is to create an accurate record of the testimony. Do not point to documents and refer to "here" or "over there." Rather, use descriptions such as, "In the upper left corner of the document" or "the curve of the second 'r' in the word 'terrible'."

When asked to examine a document, stop talking because you cannot read and talk at the same time. During any recess, politely maintain your distance from everyone. If you need to confer with counsel, do so out of sight of fact finder and opposition. Be particularly cautious of casual conversation in hallways, restrooms, and dining areas. If approached by a juror, do not engage in conversation. Report the encounter to the lawyer immediately. Throughout your testimony you must be conscious of proper breath control, upright posture, and elimination of distracting or nervous mannerisms, such as facial expressions, verbal tics, such as "ummmmm," or "okay," eye rolling, clicking a pen open and shut, or physical ticks (tapping fingers or feet).

When a witness is asked a question, the opposing attorney can raise an objection, including (but not limited to) the following reasons:

- Non-responsive
- Best evidence rule
- Compound question
- Present recollection refreshed
- Past recollection recorded
- Hearsay
- Leading question
- Argumentative or inflammatory
- Asked and answered
- Calls for speculation
- Irrelevant, immaterial, incompetent
- Lack of foundation

The Rules of Evidence provide for structure during court proceedings. Attorneys make objections when they believe the other attorney or the witness has overstepped the bounds of appropriate behavior. When an attorney objects, as the witness, your job is to stop talking immediately. Typically, you will know an objection is being made because the other attorney will preface their remarks with the word, "Objection." However, this is not always the case. As a general rule, any time you are speaking, or about to speak, and an attorney starts talking, this is your cue to stop talking. Leave it to the lawyers and the judge to sort out the appropriateness of a question or a response. Do not substitute your judgment for that of the court. At best, you will annoy the judge. At worst, your conduct could cause a mistrial. Remain silent until you are told by either the judge or the lawyer asking you questions that you may respond or not respond.

The following is a brief description of some of the most common objections.

An objection of "non-responsive" is somewhat unusual in that it objects not to the question asked, but rather the answer provided. As the word implies, an objection "non-responsive" indicates the attorney is objecting to the fact the witness did not answer the question that was asked. For example, if the question is "Do you own a watch?" the answer, "It's 4:30" is non-responsive. If asked, "Did you perform testing in this case?" answering, "It was arson" is non-responsive. The remedy for providing a non-responsive answer typically is the jury is instructed by the court to disregard the answer. Repeatedly ignoring the question presented could result in additional sanctions imposed on the witness. There may also be an objection to the answer, typically that the answer is non-responsive to the question (Q: What time is it? A: Cheesecake).

The best evidence rule is a common law rule of evidence that dates to the eighteenth century. The general rule is that secondary evidence, like a copy or facsimile, will not be admissible if the original document is available. In the eighteenth century, a copy was usually made by hand by a clerk, and the best evidence rule was predicated on the assumption that there was a significant chance of error or fraud in using a copy. In the digital age, the rule is more difficult to justify. The likelihood of actual error (as opposed to mere illegibility) through photocopying or scanning is slight because most are legible and authenticated. Further, the question remains as to what the original of an electronic communication, like email, really is.

A compound question is one that contains several components. In trial, a compound question will likely raise an objection because the witness may be unable to answer the question unambiguously. For example, if an attorney cross-examining a defendant asked, "Isn't it true that you shot your spouse in the head, then volunteered for the local battered women's shelter?" the question could not be answered with a simple yes or no. All or part of the question could be true:

- The defendant did shoot his spouse and volunteered
- The defendant did shoot his spouse but did not volunteer
- The defendant did not shoot his spouse but did volunteer
- The defendant did not shoot his spouse or volunteer

Compound questions are objectionable for several reasons, including the risk they will confuse either the witness or the trier of fact. One risk, for example, includes the risk the witness may be responding to only part of the question. Both "and" and "or" can create this problem. Once objected to and sustained, an attorney will be given the opportunity to rephrase the question into several questions, such as:

- Isn't it true you shot your spouse in the head?
- On the day your spouse was shot, did you volunteer at the homeless shelter?

Put this way, there is no ambiguity or uncertainty about what is being asked or answered.

The hearsay rule is a rule of evidence that defines hearsay and provides for both exceptions and exemptions from that rule. The hearsay rule was designed to prevent testimony by people who heard another person say something, who cannot be cross-examined on the substance of what they heard but only that they heard it. Since hearsay statements are being used to prove the truth of the matter asserted, it can be terribly damaging if the opposing party cannot cross-examine the person who uttered the statement. Technically, forensic laboratory reports are hearsay when used by themselves in court. The United States Supreme Court addressed the use of forensic laboratory reports in *Massachusetts v. Melendez-Diaz* and *New Mexico v. Bullcoming*. Broadly speaking, forensic reports are not in and of themselves admissible. However, given the volume of work performed in any given case, not to mention in the laboratory overall, it is not uncommon for a witness to forget one or more details in the file. When this happens, there are two methods lawyers can use to attempt to admit the facts contained in the file.

An attorney may attempt to refresh your present recollection (referred to as present recollection refreshed). For example, imagine you examined evidence in the lab, wrote a report, and have reviewed the file prior to testifying. You are now in court, testifying about the evidence you examined. However, imagine you cannot recall whether you examined two shotguns and a rifle, or two rifles and a shotgun. You knew the information when you reviewed the file. An attorney may attempt to refresh your recollection as follows:

Q. *Did you have the opportunity to examine the evidence in the laboratory?*
A. *Yes.*
Q. *Did you write a report based on your examination of the evidence?*
A. *Yes.*
Q. *Did you review the file before court, including your report?*
A. *Yes.*
Q. *I'm going to ask you to take a look at your report, specifically, the third paragraph on the second page. Do you see that part of your report?*
A. *Yes.*
Q. *Please read that part of your report to yourself and let me know when you are done.*
A. *I'm finished.*
Q. *After reading your report, does that refresh your recollection of the types of firearms you examined at the laboratory?*
A. *Yes.*
Q. *Please tell the jury about the firearms you examined.*

Sometimes, however, no amount of file review will jog a witness's memory. In that case, an attorney may be able to get the information in as "past recollection recorded." Assume that you used a specific setting on an instrument in your analysis. On the witness stand, you cannot remember the exact number, however, the number is part of the standard protocol.

The attorney may ask,

Q. *At the time you performed the testing, did you follow the standard protocol?*
A. *Yes.*
Q. *Did you document that setting in your notes?*

A. *(after confirming in notes) Yes.*
Q. *Does that refresh your recollection?*
A. *No. I still do not have an independent recollection of this setting.*

(Note: The attorney first tries to refresh the witness's recollection. However, just because the witness does not independently recall the information doesn't mean the information isn't admissible. The examination continues.)

Q. *Did you document that setting at the time you did the testing?*
A. *Yes.*
Q. *Is it fair to say the purpose of documenting such information is so you or another person will be able to look at the notes and determine what steps you took?*
A. *Yes.*
Q. *At the time you were documenting the testing you performed, did you take care to make accurate notes?*
A. *Yes.*
Q. *Is this a record of information you recorded in the past, closer to the time of testing?*
A. *Yes.*
Q. *And what was the setting?*
A. *According to my notes made on the day of the analysis, that value was 28.4.*

A leading question is one that suggests the answer. For example, "You were at the scene of the crime on the 7th of December, were you not?" It suggests that the witness was at the scene on the day in question. The non-leading form of this question would be, "Where were you on the 7th of December?" In essence, non-leading questions are open ended. Leading questions typically call for a yes or no answer.

Whether a leading question is proper or not depends on the relationship of the witness to the attorney asking the question. An attorney may ask leading questions of a hostile witness or on cross-examination, but not typically on direct examination. An exception to this rule occurs if a witness has been declared a hostile witness. If the court declares the witness "hostile," the attorney may ask the witness leading questions during direct examination.

When the attorney is finished with direct examination of you, he will "pass the witness," often by saying "No further questions" to the judge, or "Your witness" to the opposing attorney.

Trials are supposed to be fact-finding missions for the jury. As such, argument is reserved for closing arguments, where each lawyer takes the facts presented at trial and argues about their significance, meaning, or whether the evidence rises to the legal level of proof required, be it beyond a reasonable doubt or a preponderance of the evidence, depending on whether it is a criminal or civil trial. Questions that are argumentative are objectionable. For example, "You examined the evidence?" "And this was at your so-called independent laboratory?" The question makes the argument the laboratory is not, in fact, independent. This argument should be saved for closing argument.

Once a question has been asked and answered, attorneys should move on to another line of questioning. Sometimes, attorneys will repeat a question to highlight the answer, such as, "I want to make sure I understood your testimony. You stated you cannot determine, in this case, whether the fire was intentionally set?" This question, in and of itself, is acceptable. Usually, when a question is objected to as asked and answered, it is because an attorney is seeking a different answer than the one provided. It might look like this:

Q. *You said you couldn't determine if the fire was set?*
A. *Correct.*
Q. *So it might have been set?*
A. *Correct. I couldn't determine that.*
Q. *If someone did set it, you couldn't tell?*
A. *Yes.*
Q. *And it's also possible it wasn't set?*
A. *Correct.*

At some point, the attorney for the other side will object to this line of questioning as "asked and answered." Whether the objection will be sustained after the second question, the third, or the fourth, is up to the judge.

When an attorney asks about a hypothetical, they set the parameters. When a question calls for speculation, no such parameters have been set. Questions such as, "What was the shooter thinking when he fired into the crowd," and "How long do you think it took him to travel five miles on foot?" call for speculation, as there are variables that cannot be known to the witness. Did the person run five miles? Walk five miles? Walk three miles, run one mile, and take a nap before jogging the final mile? Without a video or eyewitnesses, this calls for speculation, not fact, and is therefore objectionable.

Witnesses are cautioned, even if there is no objection, to consider carefully any question that calls for you to speculate about things such as what was going on in someone else's mind, how long it took to travel a distance without a valid measurement, etc.

Similarly, when an attorney objects as the question assumes facts not in evidence, the question fails to set the parameters of a hypothetical. For example, assume a trial wherein the labor and delivery are at issue. At the time of the question, there has been no information about the length of the woman's labor. The question, "Couldn't several days of unattended labor result in sepsis?" assumes several days of labor. An attorney may object because of this. However, the question can easily by modified to an acceptable question by couching it as, "Dr., assume a hypothetical wherein a woman labors alone for several days. Could this result in sepsis?"

Relevancy is a judicial determination. What is important to one person or case may be of no consequence in a different circumstance. For example, the color of the car driven away from the crime scene may be relevant. The color of the car driven by the person who dropped the evidence off at the lab probably is irrelevant.

Before witnesses can testify about certain things, lawyers must lay the foundation. This includes providing the basis for admitting an expert's opinion, as well as establishing a foundation for items of evidence. To lay foundation for an expert opinion, a lawyer must establish the witness's credentials, whether based on education, training, experience, or a combination of these or other factors. To lay foundation for evidence, lawyers must ask the following:

- Do you recognize this?
- What is it?
- How do you recognize it?
- Is it in the same condition (or substantially same condition) as when you examined it?

Attorneys must also establish a chain of evidence prior to taking testimony about an item of evidence. If an expert is asked about an area where no expertise has been established, or an expert is asked about an item of evidence where it hasn't been established they examined the evidence, or that it is in the same condition, an attorney may object due to lack of foundation.

Redirect Examination

Once the attorney is finished with direct examination, the attorney representing the other side is allowed to cross-examine the witness (cross-examination is discussed further in Chapter 8). When the attorney is finished with their direct examination of you, they will "pass the witness," often by saying "No further questions" to the judge or "Your witness" to the opposing attorney.

Redirect examination occurs after cross-examination. This allows the attorney an opportunity to ask the witness to explain or qualify any answers obtained on cross-examination. Redirect examination is limited to topics discussed on cross-examination. If an attorney attempts to bring up a new area for testimony, the opposing attorney may object to that line of questioning as beyond the scope of cross-examination.

Experts frequently express frustration when an attorney either chooses not to redirect or alternatively doesn't hit every point the expert thinks should be addressed. Experts are reminded, attorneys have theories and themes of their case, which may have little or nothing to do with one or more of the finer points of the cross-examination of an individual witness—even if that witness is an expert. Consider, for example, imagine a man is on trial for beating his wife to death with a lead pipe. Imagine further, the defendant is arguing self defense. Whether a defense attorney misstated the finer points of the polymerase chain reaction, while demonstrably wrong, is of no consequence to the state's theory, which focuses on the defendant's duty to and ability to retreat, not on how DNA testing works. Thus, rather than risk alienating the jury on a technical point of no consequence, most attorneys will simply, wisely, maintain their focus on the legal issues at hand in the case and choose not to redirect on that issue.

Elements That Enhance Direct Examination

Experts and attorneys agree that certain elements make for a better witness and better testimony. Those elements include:

- The ability to coordinate verbal testimony with documentation
- Basic and complex ideas in a simple manner
- Supporting opinions with admitted evidence
- A serious but pleasant demeanor
- An observable comfort level with the material and the courtroom experience

Coordination of testimonial media involves a smooth blend of verbal testimony with charts, drawings, exhibits, and other tangible items to support the testimony. That blend becomes smoother with practice, rehearsal, and improved timing. You should build to your conclusions in a linear sense, accumulating facts and results that lead to your conclusion. It is a building block philosophy: Since A, B, and C are already established, D must be true. If prior adverse expert testimony has established certain facts or conclusions, the more of those facts and conclusions that you can use to bolster your opinions, the stronger and more reliable your opinion. Be willing to agree to the truth—just because another or opposing expert said it does not make it false.

You become a better expert witness by observing others. Watch, listen, and read. Visualize yourself as that witness: How would you handle that question or use that chart? Review your own depositions with an eye toward improving the sharpness of your answers. Watch a video of yourself testifying, if possible. Look for opportunities to sharpen your skills, your style, your technique, and your presentation. The goal is to become a more competent, persuasive, and believable witness and a more reliable resource for the justice system. Better testimonial skill is one aspect of that effort, and it is first displayed on direct examination.

Be a Teacher

The testament to your skill as an expert witness is your ability to teach. An analysis of what it takes to become a good teacher is instructive. Your instructors from high school, college, and graduate school may stand as good or bad examples of how to teach. Remembering what it is like to be a student is also key—avoid bad habits of bad teachers. Some qualities of persuasive and effective teaching are applicable to the courtroom arena. Good teachers are well informed, enthusiastic, provocative, and intellectually curious. They use examples and illustrations. They have a sense of humor. They engage their audience through eye contact. They are dedicated to their work. Good teachers engage the student with quality information, arranged sensibly and logically, in a way that encourages mental or physical participation.

Creating Instructional Materials: A Global Approach

Perhaps the most common model used for creating instructional materials is the ADDIE model. In this model, each step has an outcome that feeds into the subsequent step: Analysis, design, development, implementation, and evaluation. In the analysis phase, the particular instructional problem is clarified, the goals and objectives of the learning are detailed, and the learning environment and learner's existing knowledge and skills are identified. Questions that are addressed during the analysis phase include:

- Who is the audience and what is their background?
- What question is before them?
- What types of learning constraints exist, for example, how long will the teaching last?
- What are the delivery or media options?
- How much time does the instructor have to prepare?

The design phase deals with learning objectives, how the quality of the teaching will be assessed, presentation media and activities, content, subject matter analysis, and lesson planning. The design phase should include a logical, orderly method of identifying, developing, and evaluating a set of planned strategies targeted for attaining the project's goals. Each element of the instructional design plan needs to be executed with attention to details. These are steps used for the design phase:

- Document the project's instructional, visual, and technical design strategy, if any
- Apply instructional strategies according to the content type
- Create storyboards or outlines of the instruction for use in practice for testimony
- Design the media and presentation characteristics to be used, after consultation with the attorney
- Create and rehearse a prototype

The development phase is where the instructors create and assemble the content created in the design phase. The instructor works to develop or integrate technologies, "debug" the procedures, and review and revise the instruction plan based on feedback. During the implementation phase, the instruction is delivered according to plan. The media are deployed and the lessons provided through the chosen technologies.

After delivery, the evaluation phase consists of two parts: Formative and summative. Formative evaluation is present in each stage of the ADDIE process. Summative evaluation consists of tests designed for criterion-related referenced items and providing opportunities for feedback from the users. In testimony, feedback typically comes from three sources: Yourself, the attorney who called you, and any reviewers in the courtroom.

Experts should welcome feedback at all stages, as it makes them better witnesses. Experts may gather preliminary feedback from colleagues, coworkers, family, and friends by practicing their delivery of information prior to testifying.

Creating Instructional Materials: A Concrete Approach

An approach for presenting instructional materials developed by the U.S. Navy is represented by the acronym TOM I PASTA, which includes nine main parts:

- Title
- Objective

- Materials
- Introduction
- Presentation
- Application
- Study
- Testing
- Assignment

You can use this format when you take the witness stand for direct examination to teach what you have learned about a case to the judge, jury, or hearing panel. However, do not attempt this approach (or any approach) cold. Practice this approach ahead of time.

Presenting Complex Data

Statistical data and expert testimony can be difficult for juries, judges, and hearing panels to understand. The reasons are simple:

- The material is complex
- The topic is foreign
- The relevance of the testimony is not clear
- The presentation is boring

The presentation of statistics can be interesting if you take certain proactive steps. Studies have shown that lengthy statistical data can be vitalized by a single hypothetical case example.[5] For instance, if a statistical chart demonstrates a particular conclusion, that drab numerical summary can be brought to life by use of "factitious" example. If the summary chart of a thousand events suggests a particular incidence of drug reaction, the expert on direct could proceed as follows:

Q: Doctor, you are familiar with the chart, Exhibit A, isn't that correct?
A: Yes.
Q: How is it that you are familiar with the Exhibit?
A: I prepared it for the purposes of this trial.
Q: What does a chart like that really mean?
A: It means that if I see 1,000 patients, only 1.2 or, say, a maximum of 2 will ever experience the drug reaction that occurred in this case. In other words, the chance of this adverse reaction occurring is quite remote.

To present statistics clearly, you must explain what the statistics are based on. Explain how the information was gathered. Explain how information provides scientific or technical credibility to a proposition by numeric probability. Illustrate your presentation with lively, clear, and persuasive visual aids when possible. Finally, relate the statistics to the facts of the case at issue. Numerous studies have shown that people, including educated professionals, interpret frequencies better than percentages; people intuitively understand how to interpret frequencies better than percentages; people intuitively understand what "about 1 in 1,000" means better than "0.012 percent."[6] To present complex information takes time, thought, and careful preparation—the more complex, the more time, thought, and preparation.[7] Newspapers are written on an eighth-grade level; jurors are no differently situated than readers of the newspaper.[8] Consider modifying your testimony accordingly. Trying to explain mass spectroscopy or DNA extraction, amplification, and analysis to a group of tenth graders is different than discussing them with your colleagues.

Review Questions

1. What is direct examination?
2. What is a bailiff?
3. What is an objection?
4. What is a compound question?
5. What is hearsay?
6. What is a leading question?
7. What is the taxonomy of educational objectives?
8. What is the ADDIE model?
9. What is TOM I PASTA?

Discussion Questions

1. Why should you approach direct examination like a teacher or instructor?
2. Would you handle redirect any differently than direct examination?
3. Explain to a non-scientist friend or family member some complicated aspect of your job. What questions do they ask? What did you leave out or assume they knew?

Notes

1. Dr. Spitz, W. (testimony). *Fred Goldman et al. v. O.J. Simpson*, 43 Cal. 4th 553 (2008). November 12.

2. Welsh, A., *Strong Representations: Narrative and Circumstantial Evidence in England* (Baltimore: Johns Hopkins University Press, 1992).
3. National Institute of Justice, *Eyewitness Testimony: A Trainer's Manual for Law Enforcement* (Washington, DC: National Institute of Justice, 2003).
4. Bailiffs are the law enforcement arm of the court. They keep order in the court, serve legal process or other court documents, and take charge of juries when the court is not in session. Also, bailiffs will provide general security for the courthouse and its visitors and staff.
5. Goodman, N., Greene, E. and Loftus, E., "What Confuses Jurors in Complex Cases: Judges and Jurors Outline the Problems," *Trial*, November 1985, pp. 65–73.
6. Gigerenzer, G., *Simple Heuristics That Make Us Smart* (Oxford: ABC Research Group, Oxford University Press, 1999).
7. Pascal, Blaise, "Je n'ai fait celle-ci plus longue que parceque je n'ai pas eu le loisir de la faire plus courte" (I would have written a shorter letter, but i did not have the time), Provincial Letters: Letter XVI.
8. "Now Juries Are on Trial," *Time*, September 3, 1979.

The Visual Display of Information

7

Key Terms

Anscombe's Quartet
Chartjunk
Chewbacca Defense
Data-ink
Demonstration
Enthymemes
Graphic
Syllogism
Trial chart

Introduction

Experts tell us we learn 15 percent from what we hear and 85 percent from what we see. Therefore, you must translate complex principles into visual presentations. You must clearly demonstrate how those principles can be applied to the facts of your case. The following is a list of possible vehicles for visual presentation of technical data; these materials must be planned early in your casework:

- Drawings, for use during testimony
- Photographs, including black and white and color enlargements and slides
- Films or videos
- Charts and graphs[1]
- Time-lapse still photography
- Photographic enlargements or overhead projection of critical documents
- Parts, samples, or specimens of tests which were performed
- Microscopic examination of slides
- Models and mockups of the site
- Computer-generated or enhanced animation to demonstrate movement, time, and sequences of events

DOI: 10.4324/9781003610540-7

- Computer-enhanced displays to portray otherwise difficult-to-observe features
- Digital retouching of photographs (be sure to state that retouching has been done)
- Three-dimensional computer graphics

It is the truly great witness who uses demonstrative and graphic aids for maximum effect, working with counsel to obtain appropriate rulings to allow use or admissibility. A truly poor witness can use graphics that confuse the jury and obscure the evidence.

Visually Displaying Quantitative Information

If you have numeric information, why bother with graphics? Consider the following four sets of numbers in Table 7.1:

Table 7.1 The datasets for Anscombe's Quartet. The x values are the same for the first three datasets.

Dataset I		Dataset II		Dataset III		Dataset IV	
x	*y*	*x*	*y*	*x*	*y*	*x*	*y*
10.0	8.04	10.0	9.14	10.0	7.46	8.0	6.58
8.0	6.95	8.0	8.14	8.0	6.77	8.0	5.76
13.0	7.58	13.0	8.74	13.0	12.74	8.0	7.71
9.0	8.81	9.0	8.77	9.0	7.11	8.0	8.84
11.0	8.33	11.0	9.26	11.0	7.81	8.0	8.47
14.0	9.96	14.0	8.10	14.0	8.84	8.0	7.04
6.0	7.24	6.0	6.13	6.0	6.08	8.0	5.25
4.0	4.26	4.0	3.10	4.0	5.39	19.0	12.50
12.0	10.84	12.0	9.13	12.0	8.15	8.0	5.56
7.0	4.82	7.0	7.26	7.0	6.42	8.0	7.91
5.0	5.68	5.0	4.74	5.0	5.73	8.0	6.89

This data set is called Anscombe's Quartet.[2] The four sets of data that make up the quartet are similar in many respects. For each of the four sets:

- mean of the x values = 9.0
- mean of the y values = 7.5
- equation of the least-squared regression line is: $y = 3 + 0.5x$
- sums of squared errors (about the mean) = 110.0

- regression sums of squared errors (variance accounted for by x) = 27.5
- residual sums of squared errors (about the regression line) = 13.75
- correlation coefficient = 0.82
- coefficient of determination = 0.67

However, when the data are plotted, the differences among the data sets are obvious.

Without graphic representation, the patterns of the data sets would be lost. Imagine being an expert who has generated the equivalent of Anscombe's Quartet in your analysis but has not plotted them; you walk into court and the opposing witness has Figure 7.1 presented to the jury. Ouch.

Graphic representations of data can take many forms, from charts, to graphs, to tables, in an almost limitless array; choosing the best one can be difficult. Edward Tufte, an outstanding expert on graphic displays, states that "data graphics visually display measured quantities by means of the combined use of points, lines, a coordinate system, numbers, symbols, words, shading, and color."[3] According to Tufte, data graphics should do the following:

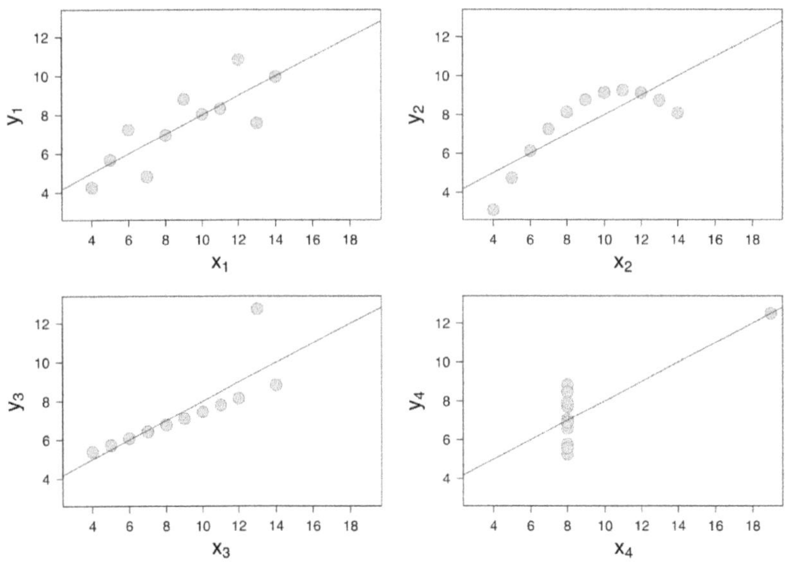

Figure 7.1 This graphic represents the four datasets defined by Francis Anscombe for which some of the usual statistical properties (mean, variance, correlation, and regression line) are the same, even though the datasets are different. (Reference: Anscombe, Francis J. (1973) Graphs in statistical analysis. American Statistician, 27, 17–21. Image sourced from Wikipedia, Used per CC BY SA 3.0, User: Avenue, subscript labels added by User: Schustz.).

- Show the data
- Get the viewer to think about the content, not the form
- Avoid distorting what the data have to say
- Make large data sets coherent
- Encourage comparison between data
- Reveal the data on several levels
- Serve a reasonably clear purpose
- Be integrated with verbal and statistical descriptions

Any visualizations to be used in court must be clear, accurate, and visually meaningful.

Data-Ink

The majority of the ink in a graphic should present the data or information the graphic is intended to show. Data-ink is the non-erasable portion of the graphic, without which the data would cease to be represented. Some graphics use nearly all of their ink on the data while others apparently hide the data beneath wells of ink. Obscuring data is easier than you might think. Take, for example, this simple data set (23, 34, 47, 51, 68, 71, 99, 105) charted in a popular spreadsheet program:

How much of the ink in this graphic presents the data (see Figure 7.2)? What could you remove and still have the data? Most of it, as it turns out (see Figure 7.3):

While not an excellent graphic (the spacing could be closer, the axes could be tighter, among others), it is certainly clearer than the previous "pyramids of power" chart that the software automatically produced. Even a simple bar graph over-represents the data six times (see Figure 7.4):

In any graphic, the amount of data-ink should be maximized and the amount of non-data-ink should be minimized or removed entirely.

Graphs, Graphics, and Comparisons in Court

After all this discussion of what not to do, what is a graphic? A graphic is a visual representation of information or data. Graphics surround us from maps, to charts, to graphs, and diagrams. What you choose to use to demonstrate your evidence to the jury is largely up to you, so a good understanding of how to arrange information is key to a successful trial chart, the name typically given to visual representations used by forensic witnesses.

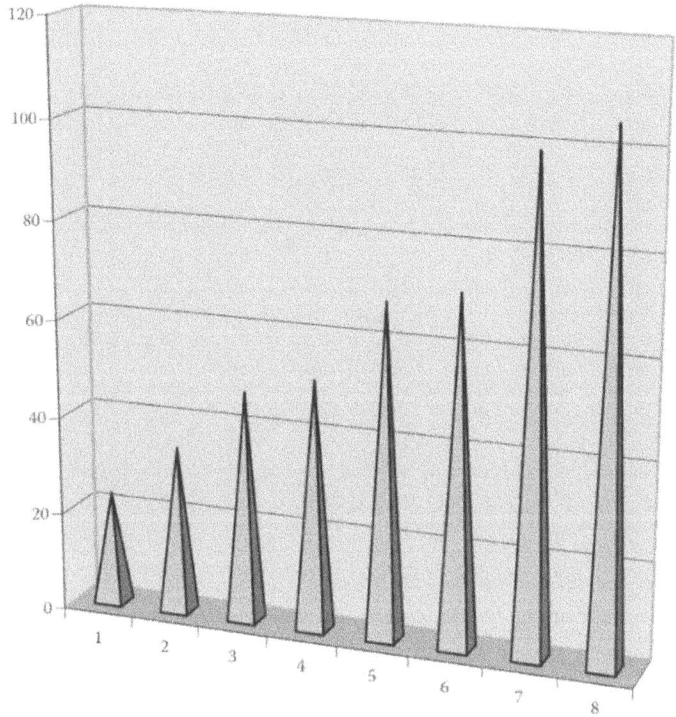

Figure 7.2 Most of the ink in this graphic goes to things other than the data.

The arrangement of the elements of a trial chart are key to getting your point across. For example, you would use the layout shown in Figure 7.5 1) to encourage comparisons within sets of items (carpet fibers vs. garment fibers, for instance). The arrangement in Figure 7.5 2) would be to encourage comparisons between sets (evidence found on the suspect and the victim, for example). Finally, the layout in Figure 7.5 3) promotes comparison of data points. Using 2) to compare items from the victim and the suspect would not help the jury to see the similarities or differences between the elements; to compare A with A, they have to visually skip over B.

Using a forensic example, review Figure 7.6 and Figure 7.7 and think of them as trial charts. This is a case of drunk driving and a breath alcohol result will be presented and most likely challenged as being insufficient compared to blood alcohol results. How would you improve on these graphics? Take a few minutes and make some notes thinking about data-ink, chartjunk, and what you want to show the jury.

You should have considered some of the following:

- Removing the background grid
- Removing the axes and the frame

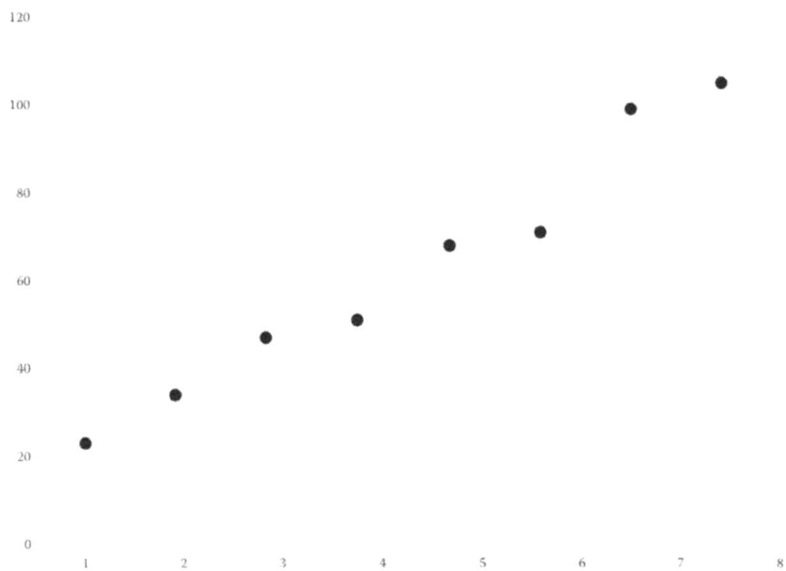

Figure 7.3 Most of the ink in this graphic is devoted to representing the data.

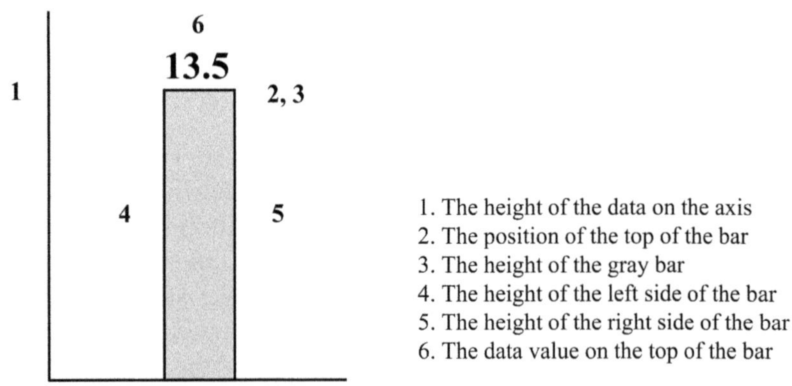

Figure 7.4 Even a seemingly innocent bar graph can massively over-represent the data.

- Decreasing the font
- Moving the label "Minutes" to below the values to provide symmetry
- Removing the data point markers; the trend is more important than any single data point

Finally, did you consider combining them into one chart? The key thing you want to emphasize with this data is the difference between blood and breath alcohol results (see Figure 7.8).

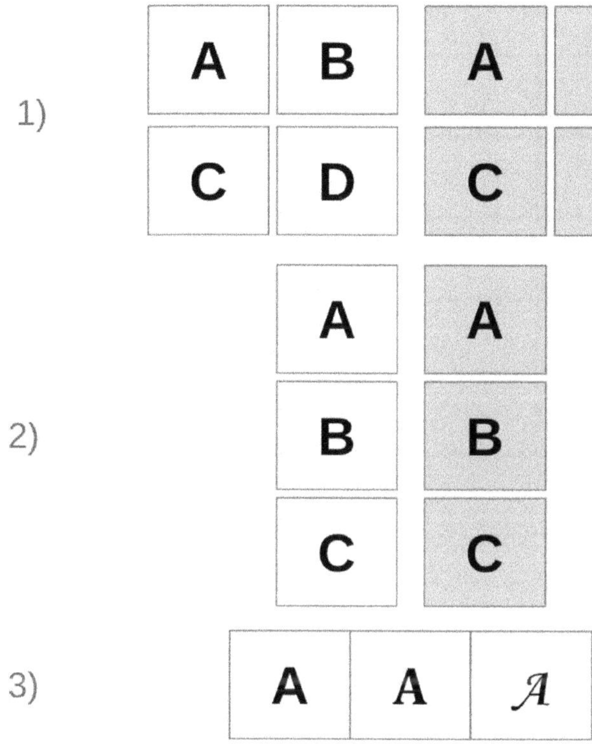

Figure 7.5 Example arrangement of comparative elements in a trial chart.

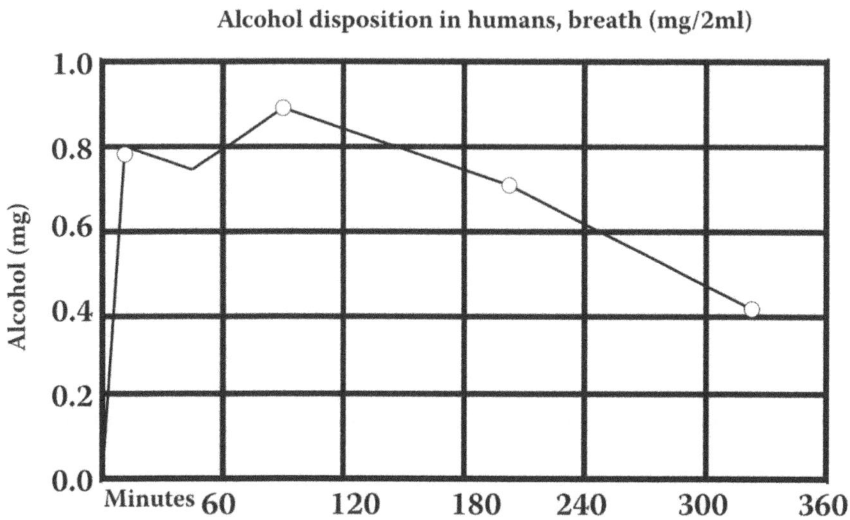

Figure 7.6 A plot of breath alcohol values.

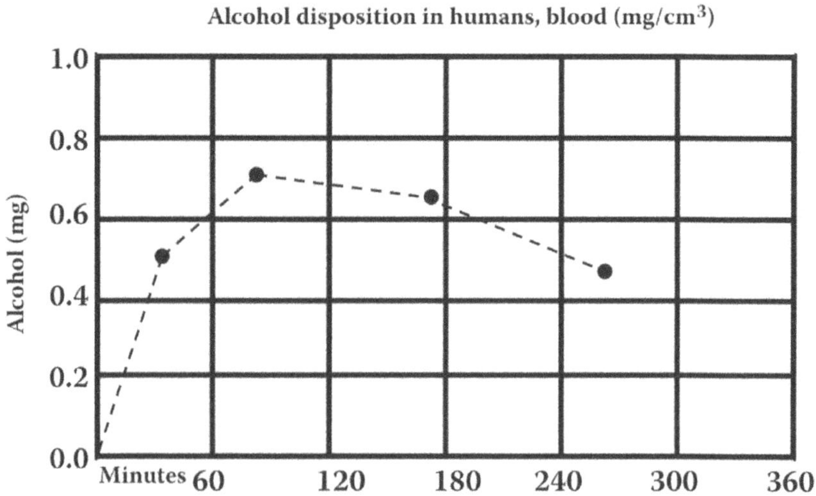

Figure 7.7 A plot of blood alcohol values.

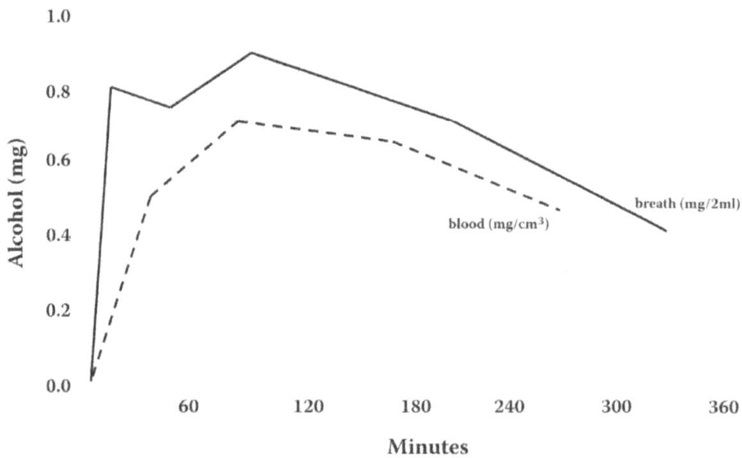

Figure 7.8 A reconfiguration of Figure 7.6 and Figure 7.7.

The jury will now see that, although the method of measuring blood alcohol content may change, the body's response is the same. This graphic will strongly support the verbal discussion of why both methods are useful. Imagine trying to support that argument without any of these graphics.

Demonstrations: If the Glove Doesn't Fit, You Must Acquit

A demonstration, a presentation of activities or events to illustrate how something happens, must be carefully considered before being performed in open court. Inherently more complicated than a static graphic, a demonstration involves the live or recorded action of the events to be displayed. If the timing is off, if something is missing, if the software seizes up, if any of a myriad things go wrong, the demonstration makes the demonstrator look unprofessional or ill-prepared.

The core of any graphic is the information presented in it. For a demonstration, it is the rational chain of events leading to an inevitable conclusion; miss a link in that chain and the argument does not work. Arguments that have unstated assumptions, or links in this analogy, are called enthymemes. The unstated assumption must be true for the premise of the argument to lead to the desired conclusion. This makes it difficult to assess the argument or perhaps even to have it be persuasive.[4] An example of an enthymeme is: Socrates is mortal because he is human. The complete argument[5] would be the classic:

All humans are mortal (assumed)
Socrates is human
Therefore, Socrates is mortal

Enthymemes are not necessarily invalid but they can be illogical yet persuasive. The best modern example of this is the argument Johnnie Cochran offered in defense of O.J. Simpson: "The glove doesn't fit [the defendant], so you must acquit."[6] The glove in question is one found at the scene soaked in the victims' blood and dried by the time it was collected. The prosecutors asked Simpson to try on the evidence glove—not a clean new one as would have been the case prior to the crime—in front of the jury. Simpson's struggling to fit his rubber-gloved hand (for safety reasons) into the dried, shrunken glove left an indelible impression on the jury and one that Cochran fully exploited. The extended argument would be:

If any evidence does not fit the defendant, then acquittal is required (assumed)
The glove doesn't fit the defendant
The glove is evidence
Therefore, you must acquit the defendant

More is unstated in this argument, even in this extended form, than is stated. For example, how "fit" is determined, which glove is being discussed (the one from the scene, the one the perpetrator used, a clean one, etc.). Hiding premises can be an effective way to deflect criticism of questionable reasoning. Hiding premises is not, however, how you should prepare your court demonstrations.

Each link in your argument should be transparent, clearly stated, and stoutly connected to the premises that precede and follow it. Discuss the demonstration with the attorney ahead of time (no surprises!). Practice and rehearse your demonstrations multiple times to make sure it works properly in the allotted time. Know what materials and resources you will need in the courtroom and either take them or have them ready when you arrive. Demonstrations can be effective but they can also be disasters if they are not thought through, planned, prepared, and executed properly.

Conclusion

Graphics can greatly enhance your testimony—they can also distract from it. Plan ahead on how to use graphic displays of information to support your testimony. Think about what is the essence of what you want to show to the jury. Consider the comparisons you want them to make. Are your graphics clear, concise, and free from chartjunk? Have you maximized the data-ink? Review and rehearse any demonstrations you plan to do; rehearse them again and again to make sure they work. You will encounter enough surprises in court without inadvertently creating them yourself.

Review Questions

1. What is Anscombe's Quartet?
2. What is data-ink?
3. What is chartjunk? Find a good "bad" example in a news or journal article.
4. What is a graphic?
5. What is a trial chart? Is it different from a graphic?
6. What is a demonstration?
7. What is an enthymeme?
8. What is the "Chewbacca Defense"?
9. What is a syllogism? Is it the same as an argument?
10. Why would you, as an expert, use a graphic in court?

Discussion Questions

1. Take the example of chartjunk you found for Review Question 3. Find the original data or estimate the data as best you can. Re-format the

graphic using the principles in this chapter. What did you change? What did you keep (data-ink)? Why?
2. Although it is not covered in this chapter, think about color in a graphic. When do you have to use it and when could you get away with black and white or gray tones?
3. Consider a scenario where a demonstration you planned to use in court encounters a technical malfunction during your testimony. How would you handle this situation to maintain your credibility and effectively convey the intended information to the jury?

Notes

1. See, for example, Rule 106, Federal Rules of Evidence, specifically allowing, if not encouraging, use of such summary charts and graphs.
2. Anscombe, F.J., "Graphs in Statistical Analysis," *American Statistician*, 27 (1973), pp. 17–21.
3. Tufte, E., *The Visual Display of Quantitative Information* (Chesire, CT: Graphics Press, 1983).
4. Heinrichs, J., *Thank You for Arguing* (New York: Three Rivers Press, 2007).
5. This is technically a syllogism, an argument in which one proposition is inferred from the previous two, but a proper treatment of this topic is beyond the scope of this book. The interested reader is directed to, Priest, G., *Logic: A Very Short Introduction* (Oxford: Oxford University Press, 2000).
6. Wonderfully parodied in the South Park episode, "Chef Aid." In the episode, Johnnie Cochran defends a character using the Chewbacca Defense, consisting of nonsensical arguments meant to confuse a jury. Cochran states, "I have one final thing that I want you to consider. Ladies and gentlemen, this is Chewbacca. Chewbacca is a Wookiee from the planet Kashyyyk. But Chewbacca lives on the planet Endor. Now think about it; that does not make sense! ... Why would a Wookiee, an eight-foot tall Wookiee, want to live on Endor, with a bunch of two-foot tall Ewoks? That does not make sense! But more importantly, you have to ask yourself: What does this have to do with this case? Nothing. Ladies and gentlemen, it has nothing to do with this case! ... If Chewbacca lives on Endor, you must acquit! The defense rests." A workshop was held at the American Academy of Forensic Sciences meeting in 2006 about the Chewbacca Defense.

Cross-Examination

8

Key Terms

Foundation
Frontloading
Historic hysteric gambit
Hypothetical questions
Learned treatise
"Yes, but" answer

Introduction

There are some specific things you can do to prepare yourself for cross-examination. Most obvious are those that have been previously discussed in this text. All those devices and ideas serve to enhance your credibility as an expert witness. As your credibility is enhanced, cross-examination threats are diminished. In truth, most cross-examination "threats" exist only in the minds of the novice witness. Experienced experts are aware they have no dog in the fight. They come to court prepared, with their conclusions based on earnest effort, experience, testing, and data. Being questioned about their findings should not be cause for consternation.

That said, there are specific things you can do to make yourself more ready and less vulnerable to cross-examination. Your resume must accurately reflect what you have actually accomplished, not what you wish you had done. Do not exceed the bounds of your own expertise. In taking on assignments and in answering questions, do not venture beyond the areas in which you are professionally qualified. The temptation is great to move into areas in which you are not qualified. Your image and credibility will be enhanced by sticking to your field of knowledge, training, and experience. Whatever investigative steps you have taken must be completed and fully documented. The thoroughness of your preparation to testify will be exemplified by your direct examination. Accurate investigation creates a dense fabric of fact that becomes difficult to penetrate on cross-examination. Further, strict adherence to scientific principles, regardless of whose position they favor, often reduces the length of cross-examination. Consider:

DOI: 10.4324/9781003610540-8

Q. *Is it possible another gun was used to fire this bullet?*
A. *It is highly unlikely.*
Q. *But it's possible?*
A. *I can't imagine that's the case.*
Q. *Are you testifying this bullet could only have been fired from this gun to the exclusion of all other guns on the planet?*
A. *Well, I didn't say that …*
Q. *So it's possible that another gun fired the weapon.*
A. *Yes.*

This lengthy exchange could have been avoided if the expert had just answered the question with a "yes" the first time. Experts who wish to be considered independent need to display this independence at all times.

Cross-Examination: Friend or Foe?

Most forensic experts dread cross-examination and with good reason: It can be very unpleasant. In reality, with planning and patience, even a vigorous cross-examination can be weathered with your integrity and results intact. If you are believable, stick to the facts you know and can support, and as long as you have done your homework, your abilities will be obvious. Psychological persuasion conveyed by body language, repetition of theme, dress, and demeanor all add to your positive image. The smooth, solid presentation you made on direct examination must be maintained throughout cross-examination. Similarly, the respect shown to one side must be shown to the other. This holds true both in your preparedness, your attitude, your demeanor, and your willingness to answer the questions posed.

Witnesses who are certain of their own effort and preparation with the data to back it up are generally questioned cautiously on cross-examination. The cross-examining attorney quickly senses your truthful and positive answers. Part of the stimulation of a classroom setting is the ability to field questions from students. The skill with which those questions are responded to is often the mark of a great teacher. Your function as an "expert witness teacher" is merely an extension of that exercise. The cross-examiner who probes your qualifications, preparation, conclusions, and opinions will press you for answers.

One of the major opportunities for attorneys during cross-examination is to highlight their theory by reviewing prior testimony. In some cases, prior testimony may be used to further make the point. See the following:

Q: You were trying to imply to this jury that that imprint was a Silga sole, weren't you?
A: No. I testified I couldn't determine that.

Q: Oh. Okay. You went a little bit further than what you testified to in the criminal case, didn't you?
A: No. I said exactly the same thing that I said in the criminal trial.
Q: All right. Let's go to page 32,842 of the criminal testimony, lines 12 through 17.
[Reading]
Q: My understanding is, there was insufficient detail present to call it one way or the other as to those marks, whether they're a footprint or not, in the Bronco?
A: I couldn't associate them with the sole to sole, yes. That was your answer, right?
A: Yes.
Q: And you weren't trying to imply to this jury that that was a Silga sole when you put the overlay over the board?
A: No, I was not.[1]

Here, the witness is confident in his wording and what he meant; this kind of confidence comes from experience, good methods, and a cool head.

During your professional career, you might have written articles, books, or reports. In addition, you might have testified in deposition or at trial on prior occasions. Your personal library should include reprints of every article you have ever published and every deposition or court transcript of your testimony. The attorney for whom you are testifying is entitled to know about your prior opinions. In addition to alerting you and the parties for whom you act to areas of cross-examination, your prior writings and testimony can supply positive support or rebuttal material for cross-examination. When asked about prior testimony, where the attorney suggests you testified differently, follow these three simple steps:

- Don't panic
- Take the time to review the facts and testimony referenced
- Consider whether the current case is the same or different from the prior case

All of this should be done prior to responding to the question.

Know the Attorney's Goals

Laying Foundation

Before discussion about the goals of cross-examination in general, a basic discussion about foundation is in order. An attorney is not allowed to ask you about an exhibit if it has not yet been introduced into evidence. Unless the parties stipulate to a piece of evidence's admission, the attorney seeking to introduce the evidence must "lay foundation" for its admission. Care should be taken to listen and only answer the questions asked during foundation. The questions are, generally:

- Do you recognize this document/item/report/photograph? This answer to this should be yes or no. That's all.
- How do you recognize it? Perhaps you examined it, wrote it, or took the picture. Limit your response to how you recognize it.
- What is it? It is a report, a gun, a photo. For this question, resist the urge to launch into a paragraph detailing your findings. Just answer with what the piece of evidence is.
- Is it in substantially the same condition as it was when you wrote it/examined it/read it? Again, the answer should be yes or no. That's it. If it is not in the same condition, wait until asked to explain what is different.

Following this series of questions, the attorney will offer the evidence for admission. Opposing counsel may choose to object to its admission. The judge then decides whether or not it is admissible. Only after the item is admitted should you be offering testimony about it.

Cross-Examination Techniques

Professor James W. McElhaney suggests eight fundamental techniques that attorneys typically employ to cross-examine an expert witness:[2]

- Make the expert your witness; highlighting evidence favorable to their theory
- Attack the field of expertise; show lack of recognition of the professional field
- Attack the witness's qualifications; establish gaps in the professional resume
- Expose the witness's bias; give reasons why testimony is slanted
- Attack the witness's fact basis; investigation was inadequate or the witness did not have access to all the facts in the case
- Change the hypothetical used on direct; vary the facts to support a different theory if use of the hypothetical question is the basis for expert opinion
- Impeach the witness with learned treatises and journals; any recognized text, authoritative in nature, can be used to cross-examine

- Attack the witness head on; find prior contra-writings by the witness

The following cases show how opposing counsel attempts to achieve these goals during cross-examination. Even if the examples are not in your field, notice the pattern, the sequence, the intent of the questions; these will be instructive to you as you learn about cross-examination.

Making the Expert Their Witness

In an action involving construction of a golf course in a residential neighborhood, the applicant's expert testified that, in his opinion, the perimeter fence around the golf course would not be unsightly. He based his conclusion on the fact that other fences at nearby golf courses, which he had photographed, did not appear to disturb neighborhood aesthetics. Cross-examination was designed to make the witness support the opposition.

Q: Do you agree, Mr. Witness, that the fence will be at least 40 feet high?
A: Yes.
Q: It will be supported by telephone pole-size support columns?
A: That's true.
Q: The fence is to be made of chicken wire, is that correct?
A: That's correct.
Q: And the fence will border residential property for approximately 300 yards, is that also correct?
A: Yes.
Q: Do you agree the chicken wire and telephone pole structure will be twice as high as any of the residences in the neighborhood?
A: I can't say for sure.
Q: Well, the houses are all one-story houses, are they not?
A: Yes.
Q: Is there any other structure like the one you have described anywhere in the neighborhood at this time?
A: No.
Q: And the homes have been there for years, isn't that true?
A: Yes, many years.

The objective of the questioning was to emphasize that the fence was out of character with the residential homes in the neighborhood. In effect, the witness, through the cross-examination, supported the opponents. The adverse effect could have been avoided if other tall structures in the area could have been identified. Of course, it is possible no other tall structures are in the area. If the witness is offering an opinion, such as in this case, the witness should have considered such arguments and addressed them in their report. Even if not included in the report, a good expert will consider counterarguments and be prepared to respond to them. Perhaps the expert would note the chicken wire is mostly air and difficult to see, for example.

Attacking the Expert's Field of Expertise

In attacking your field of expertise, the effort is to show there is little or no scientific, technical, professional, or other recognized basis to support your testimony.

Q: Dr. Jones, your field of expert testimony is environmental epidemiology, is that correct?
A: That's correct.
Q: Is it true, doctor, that there is no college or university in the United States that now offers a degree in environmental epidemiology?
A: That's correct.
Q: As a matter of fact, doctor, isn't it true there is no college or university in the world that offers a degree in environmental epidemiology?
A: That's correct.
Q: Isn't it correct, doctor, that there are no national boards that deal exclusively with the subject of environmental epidemiology?
A: That is correct.
Q: Isn't it correct, doctor, that there are no national associations that deal exclusively with the subject of environmental epidemiology?
A: That is correct.
Q: Isn't it correct, doctor, that there are no professional societies that deal exclusively with the subject of environmental epidemiology?
A: That is correct.

The fact that there is no degree in the subject and no professional association dealing exclusively with the area of expertise does not disqualify you to state opinions. However, the question has now been raised as to whether there is such a specialty field as environmental epidemiology. This is called "frontloading." The sting should have been anticipated and brought out during direct examination, not left for a cross-exam bombshell.

Attacking the Expert's Qualifications

An attack on the witness's qualifications can cover many aspects of the resume.

Q: Mr. Smith, it appears from your professional resume you attended the University of Wisconsin. Is that correct?
A: Yes, that's correct.
Q: Mr. Smith, in your resume it doesn't say what degree you received from the University of Wisconsin. Is that because you did not receive a degree?
A: The work toward my undergraduate degree was almost completed when I left the university.
Q: Mr. Smith, isn't it correct that you did not receive a degree from the University of Wisconsin?
A: Yes.
Q: As a matter of fact, Mr. Smith, isn't it correct that you never received a degree from any college or university in the United States?
A: Yes, that's correct.
Q: And isn't it also correct that you have been practicing as a professional engineer without being licensed in any state of the United States to practice that profession?
A: Yes.

While the witness did not attempt to conceal the absence of professional qualifications in his resume, the cross-examiner is making him seem unqualified to the jury. If the problem had been explored on direct examination, the thunder would have been taken from the cross-examiner. Some attorneys will ask directly, "What will the other side attack you on," when meeting with an expert before putting them on the stand. You should be prepared to answer this question, based on prior experience and common sense.

Attacking the Factual Basis for the Expert's Conclusions

In an effort to attack the factual basis of testimony, the attorney could attempt to show any of the following:

- You are not familiar with the scene of the events. Your examinations are not really scientific.
- You have not examined the actual product in question. You made no measurements.
- The measurements you did make are wrong. You carried out no tests.
- The tests you did carry out were not relevant, incorrectly applied, or had no standards.
- You were not in a position to observe the events. Your opinion is based on secondhand information.
- Your opinion is based on incomplete information.

One of the authors (MMH) had an attorney once attempt to dismiss his entire profession by responding to the answer, "I looked at the evidence in question," with, "Isn't that *all* you experts do—just *look at things*?!?" and slamming his notes down on the podium. Such attacks go nowhere if you have done your homework and keep a cool head.

The Use of Hypotheticals

Use of hypothetical questions is still a valid method of examination. The technique on cross-examination is to insert into a hypothetical question facts that could lead you to reach a conclusion opposite to that tendered on direct examination. Pay close attention to the form of the hypothetical question and do not be afraid to hedge your answers. The phrase "Assuming the facts in this case …" is a signal that the attorney wants you to make the same assumptions he is making (but may not be stating), as in the following case.

In an action involving an alleged defective setting of a ski binding which failed to release, a technician rendered an opinion that the binding had been too tight for the weight and ability of the claimant. On cross-examination, the defense attempted to establish that the claimant had lied about his skiing ability and his weight. The following exchange occurred:

Q: Isn't it correct that unless you are advised accurately as to the skier's ability and the skier's weight, you can't make the proper adjustment on the ski binding?
A: That's correct.
Q: If, instead of being an intermediate skier, the claimant was only a beginner, would that make a difference to the installing technician?
A: Yes.
Q: If the skier said he weighed 150 pounds when in fact he weighed 175 pounds, would that make any substantial difference in the adjustment?
A: Of course.
Q: For the sake of my examination, Mr. Technician, I want you to assume that the plaintiff told the ski binding technician he was an intermediate skier when in fact he was a beginning skier. I want you to further assume that the claimant stated he weighed 150 pounds when in fact he weighed 175. Now, with that information, what would the proper binding setting have been, assuming those facts?

The objective of the questioning was to create a set of facts that accorded with the defense view of the plaintiff's conduct. As the witness, your job is to consider the question and answer it.

Notice the witness's ease of requesting clarification in the following example of a complex hypothetical question:[3]

Q	*(by defense attorney):* In terms of your examination and determination of where everybody was in this reconstruction. If in fact the internal jugular vein was the first vein severed, and if, in fact, it bled down his left side and down his pants and down into his boot, you would agree that he would still have the ability to fight off an attacker for a period of time, 5 minutes or longer, true?
Opposing Counsel:	Objection. Assumes facts not in evidence, Your Honor.
The Court:	Overruled. Hypothetical question.
The Witness:	Are you asking, if I may, so I can understand the question, are you asking me whether, with a severed jugular vein, he could still fight for 5 minutes? Is that what you're asking me?

Particularly when faced with a hypothetical, clarifying the hypothetical universe is essential to maintaining your credibility.

Using a Learned Treatise

Attacking you by use of an authoritative publication is one of the most effective devices in the cross-examiner's toolkit. This is often referred to as the learned treatise.

In a case involving dissolution of a marriage, a rehabilitation counselor testified for the wife concerning her alleged inability to return to the job market because of the psychological trauma she had sustained from the divorce proceeding. A series of quotes were read from a text to the testifying witness that suggested the type of trauma being used to support the testimony was not supportable. After four quotes had been read, the witness asked the examining attorney the name of the publication. To the witness's surprise, the attorney told the witness that the quotes had been extracted from his own technical writing published within the preceding year. The court found the wife able to return to the job market. The lesson is obvious: Know what you have written previously—everything you have written—and know it cold, and be aware of what is authoritative.

FRE 803(18) states that you as an expert do not have to recognize a learned treatise as authoritative to be cross-examined about it. At least in the federal courts, if any expert witness testifies that a particular treatise is authoritative, you, as a testifying witness, may be examined about it.

An Attack on the Expert's Conclusions

A direct attack on your position is difficult to undertake, yet the effort will be made in a proper case. On occasion, you may be tempted to maintain a position of absolute certainty even in the face of overwhelming contradictions. That dogged adherence to a position can destroy your credibility.

In a case involving valuation of real property, the expert stated that his task was to place himself "on the piece of property 10 years prior" and attempt to determine value in that hypothetical stance. Cross-examination and other evidence revealed that the expert had not contacted the actual buyer, another appraiser, or the zoning official, all of whom dealt with the property 10 years before. All three of those individuals testified that the expert's opinion of value was substantially incorrect.

Nevertheless, in the face of that overwhelming contrary testimony, the expert stood fast. He maintained that he was in a better position to value the property 10 years after the fact than the three knowledgeable persons had been at the time. Steadfast adherence to an untenable position served to erode the witness's credibility. This expert can expect to be cross-examined on this incident for years to come.

Testing the Entire Field

The question as to whether you will be allowed to testify may not come up until trial. Under the FREs, the trial judge determines the qualifications of witnesses.[4] The test may be whether the scientific principles you rely on are considered reliable enough to support expert opinion. Attacks on your field of scientific expertise should not be overlooked by you as you prepare to testify, if the area of testimony has not yet reached scientific or professional acceptance or recognition. Attorneys may attack a discipline with historical anecdotes that are no longer true, ideas like phlogiston in chemistry or Lamarck's theory of inheritance through acquired traits. The attorney will then try to make your discipline look silly or make modern ideas seem as threadbare as the old discarded ones. This is known as the historic hysteric gambit.[5] The best way to counter this attack is to know the history of your discipline and understand your methods as completely as possible.

However, in some disciplines, particularly in forensic science, the evolution is going the other way. Disciplines that were once considered rock solid have been called into question by the National Academy of Sciences 2009 publication "Strengthening Forensic Science: A Path Forward" and the President's Council of Advisors on Science and Technology's Report to President Obama entitled, *Forensic Science In Criminal Courts: Ensuring Scientific Validity of Feature-Comparison Methods.* An expert should be familiar with criticism of their discipline. Among the most dangerous of questions is the hypothetical question. This is a question that proposes an imaginary situation incorporating facts about the case. Hypothetical questions can be answered only in terms of their validity, not if they make sense. For example, a person may ask: Would you drink the Atlantic Ocean if it were lemonade? To answer this question, you have to assume that the Atlantic Ocean is made of lemonade, so you have to answer only as to whether or not you would drink it. Saying "But the ocean is not lemonade" is not an appropriate response; you can only respond with answers like "yes," "no," or "depending on if enough sugar has been added." The attorney states a factual foundation (often based on disputed facts in the case) and asks the expert to draw conclusions based on the hypothetical foundation. The hypothetical question includes only facts already in evidence. Do not assume that the facts are true. Hypothetical questions are slippery things because of the (often unspoken) assumptions being made. Be willing to ask about certain facts and clarify the question.

Reducing Vulnerability to Cross-Examination

Certain areas of weakness attend some expert testimony. Those areas will certainly be the grounds for attack by a cross-examining attorney. Knowing the areas of jeopardy will help you prepare in advance for the cross-examination.

Is your opinion based in whole or in part on judgment as opposed to measurable fact? It is always proper for cross-examination to probe the basis for your well-established conclusions. If that basis is technical and scientific testing, you will not be vulnerable. However, if subjective judgment and opinion are the sole basis for your opinion, you are vulnerable. Consider two examples. A chemical test involves mixing a compound and then adding a measured number of drops of reagent to turn the compound from pink to blue. The exact number of drops necessary to cause the color change constitutes a specific scientific measurement. No judgment or opinion attends this test. The results can be documented with laboratory protocol and photographs. In a more subjective example, valuation of motor vehicles requires an orderly examination of each vehicle against a 50-point checklist. Each item on the checklist is graded from 1 to 10. Each of the 50 items requires judgment based upon observation. True, an expert's observation is more valid than that of the average person. However, judgment is the key word. This valuation would be considered a major area for cross-examination.

Is your opinion based upon input from others? You are to testify as an orthopedic surgeon. The issue is the extent of a fracture sustained in a fall. The radiologist's report suggests to you a compound comminuted fracture with

30 bone fragments at the fracture site. You testify to that effect. However, by cross-examination it is established your testimony is based on the radiology report. As an orthopedist, you may not be able to identify 30 bone fragments from the x-ray, but ordinary practice allows you to rely on the radiologist's report. You must be ready to defend your reliance as customary in your field.

Cognitive bias cannot be denied. Instead, be prepared to describe the steps taken to reduce the potential impact of cognitive bias. Acknowledging cognitive bias exists, but not in you personally, doesn't serve you. Instead, it may lead the jury to question your credibility on this and other statements you have made.

Have you made prior inconsistent statements? The questioner will ask about whatever you have written and testified to in the past. Aggressive cross-examining counsel will comb those written materials for inconsistencies.

Does your behavior suggest insecurity? The skillful cross-examining attorney will observe you carefully. If you have your hand near your mouth or face, you may be withholding information, according to the attorney's way of thinking. If you flush or your hand trembles, you may feel insecure. If you hesitate and stammer or fumble through papers and files, you may feel a lack of confidence in your own ability. Skillful examining attorneys sense a weak, inadequately prepared, or unsure witness. When that sixth sense is activated, they will move in for the kill. Your best option is to agree—up to a point—and wait for the right moment to counteract the line of questioning:

Q: If we did a tape lift, say, on that chair, might we catch one of your hairs?
A: It's possible.
Q: Possible to catch one of the fibers on your shirt?
A: That's also possible.
Q: And if I came up and sat in that very same chair, might those—might that hair and fiber get transferred to my jacket?
A: That's possible.
Q: And then if I sat down at the counsel table, might those fibers get transferred to the chair?
A: That's also possible, yes.
Q: And the hairs?
A: Yes.
Q: And then if Mr. Clarke sat in the chair, might those fibers then get transferred to Mr. Clarke?
A: That could happen, yes.
Q: And if he walked them into his office might they travel to his office?
...

The basic tenet of cross-examination for the attorney is control of the witness. This is done by crafting leading questions. This is consistent with the rules that govern cross-examination. You should expect it. You should also focus on answering the question with a yes or a no. An expert who is well prepared, did the work, documented the work, and has conclusions supported by data and science should have no fear of a series of leading questions from opposing counsel.

However, there may be times when a simple yes or no just won't do. Note: These times will be rare. If you find yourself annotating every answer, you may not be listening carefully to the questions. To the question "Mr. Expert, isn't it correct that traffic lights sequence green to yellow to red?" The easy answer is "Yes," but the better answer may be "Yes, unless there is a malfunction," if there has been a malfunction in the case at hand.

When the attorney asks a potentially damaging question, use the same air of certainty that you evidenced on direct examination. An answer like "While that may be true in a vacuum, my analysis shows …" does three things. First, you have signaled the attorney who subpoenaed you to revisit this issue on redirect. Second, you have shown your credibility in a forthright, unapologetic manner. Finally, it helps you avoid the "Yes, but" answer where an attorney may stop you after you say "Yes …" with a curt "Thank you!" By saying yes, you have linguistically satisfied the requirement for answering the question; therefore, you may not get a chance to explain your answer (the attorney may not want the jury to hear it). By saying "While that may be true …," you have not yet fully answered the question and need to continue to have your answer make sense.

Have you made sure your language is understandable and that you translate technical terms? After you have answered the question before you—stop! Do not tell everything you know about the subject. Do not annotate with little known facts. If possible, have the attorney prepare summaries of relevant facts and documents rather than providing the documents or client statements. This ensures the attorney is familiar with the topic. Work with the attorney to identify potential areas of cross-examination. Your careful preparation will allow you to participate in cross-examination in a meaningful way. Make sure the theories on which you rely rest on a reliable foundation, are based on scientifically valid principles, and are relevant to the case.

Understand What Happens Next

After direct and cross-examination, the attorney who did the direct exam will have the opportunity to do something called "redirect." It allows the attorney who called you to testify to ask additional questions to follow up on the cross-examination. Often, experts make an effort during cross to signal the attorney who called them to "loop back" to a particular area of testimony. Experts are advised these signals are not lost on opposing counsel or the jury. For witnesses claiming independence, it signals an agenda from someone who claims to be unbiased.

Additionally, what is important to the expert may not be what is important to the attorneys. Attorneys who try cases create a theme and theory which you may or may not be privy to. Do not take offense if an attorney doesn't follow up on redirect on an issue you think is important.

Conclusion

Be alert to the eight fundamental goals of cross-examination. By knowing the objectives of cross-examination, you can use the questioning process to solidify your position. Objectives of cross-examination include use of your testimony as a springboard for the cross-examiner's own expert. The cross-examination may seek to use your testimony to contradict other experts on your side or to obtain information beneficial to the cross-examiner's case. However, your preparation, credibility, and positive demeanor will blunt the challenge afforded by cross-examination.

The usual admonition for cross-examining counsel is to stop when you are ahead, use restraint, and not overplay. These same admonitions are equally true for you as the expert witness undergoing cross-examination. Do not overplay the expert role. Do not overemphasize your superior knowledge. Be accurate with the facts. Be firm without being an advocate. Maintain control of the situation.

Review Questions

1. What is a learned treatise?
2. What is one of the major opportunities that cross-examination presents for an attorney?
3. Name four ways an attorney could try to attack the factual basis of your testimony.
4. What is a "yes, but" answer?
5. What is the historic hysteric gambit?
6. How should you act toward an attorney on cross-examination?
7. Why is cross-examination even necessary, legally speaking?

8. What are the functions of cross-examination?
9. What are the best ways to prepare for a vigorous cross-examination?
10. When you finish with cross-examination, are you finished with testimony?

Discussion Questions

1. How is cross-examination like direct examination? How are they different?
2. Think about your demeanor on direct examination and then on cross-examination. What might be some ways to calm yourself if you get nervous about cross-examination?
3. Why are experts nervous about cross-examination? How could you avoid that nervousness?

Notes

1. Bodziak, W. (testimony). *Fred Goldman et al. v. O.J. Simpson*, 43 Cal. 4th 553 (2008). November 27.
2. McElhaney, J.W., "Expert Witnesses," *ABA Journal*, 75 (March 1989), pp. 98–99.
3. Dr. Spitz, W. (testimony). *Fred Goldman et al. v. O.J. Simpson*, 43 Cal. 4th 553 (2008). November 12.
4. Federal Rules of Evidence, *Rule 104(a): McCormick on Evidence*, 2nd ed., Vol. 53 (Minnesota: West Publishing Company, 1972), p. 121.
5. Brodsky, S.L., *Testifying in Court: Guidelines and Maxims for the Expert Witness* (Washington, DC: American Psychological Association, 2004).

Ethics

9

Key Terms

Alterations
Ethics
Normative ethics

Introduction

Ethics refer to the values and customs of a person or group. The topic covers the analysis and use of concepts such as right and wrong, good and evil, and personal and professional responsibility. When people speak of ethics, typically they mean normative ethics, the study of the moral standards and behaviors that help to determine what is meant by, for example, right, wrong, unethical, and immoral. People and groups articulate what good actions and behaviors they expect from others.

Four categories of ethical problems plague the use of expert witnesses in the dispute resolution process. The first has to do with unethical conduct of forensic witnesses. The second relates to admissibility of expert testimony. The third addresses negligent performance of expert service. The fourth area concerns interprofessional relations. Examination of problems and solutions provides you with guidance for future conduct, keeping in mind always that objectivity is for the expert and advocacy is for the attorney. American law schools require a course in professional responsibility covering not only ethics but matters of professionalism as they relate to practicing law. 48 of the 50 states require attorneys to sit for and pass the Multistate Professional Responsibility Examination (MPRE) before they can practice law. Similarly, the topic of ethics is required in undergraduate and graduate forensic science programs accredited by the Forensic Science Educational Program Accreditation Commission (FEPAC, at www.aafs.org).

 DOI: 10.4324/9781003610540-9

What Is Unethical Conduct?

Proportionately speaking, only rarely are expert witnesses actually found culpable for preparing fraudulent, false, or imagined scientific, technical, or professional research. Unfortunately, those cases attract a tremendous amount of attention and bring massive disfavor to an otherwise honored profession. The horror stories circulating in legal and forensic fields about experts who falsify data to support either a prosecution or defense posture in a criminal case are all too well known today. The use of false DNA, blood, alcohol, or chemical substance testing resulting in wrongful incarceration of accused defendants stands as the most reprehensible of all forensic witness abuses. However, falsification of credentials runs a close second. Finally, in some cases, a forensic witness's testimony is so inadequate as to justify exclusion at trial.

Unethical experts may tender testimony to the court based upon supposed scientific, technical, or professional findings and research when they in fact did not do the work represented by their report. Often others had actually done the work, but not necessarily under proper supervision, in which case the testimony should have been excluded.

The courts are sometimes faced with the problem of forged, altered, or otherwise falsified documents, data, or lab reports, supporting supposed expert testimony. In those situations, when exposed, based upon the crucible of cross-examination, the resulting exclusion of expert testimony seems most appropriate. Sanctions should also be imposed by the courts on both witnesses and attorneys who were informed beforehand of the hoax. For attorneys, the presentation of evidence known to be false is a serious ethical violation. The state Board of Professional Responsibility may very well also discipline the lawyer. For the testifying expert, offering false testimony is perjury, which carries with it both criminal and civil consequences. No case is so important that it is worth compromising one's integrity, not to mention, risking jail or prison time.

If an expert either willfully ignores the actual facts of the case or is deprived access to the facts by overenthusiastic counsel, the testimony of the expert should be excluded. Sometimes an expert witness will distinguish prior testimony in a similar case because it does not particularly fit facts and circumstances of the present case. Such a matter of inconsistent testimony, while totally unprofessional, is often exposed in the courtroom by aggressive cross-examination. It is hoped this kind of chicanery will be reduced in frequency from our courts and dispute resolution processes as cross-examining skills become more articulate, professional grievance practices become more stringent, and the internet makes discovery of prior positions of the expert more accessible.

Occasionally expert witnesses display a lack of knowledge or professional competence to render the opinions that are sought. In those circumstances, the likely result is that expert testimony will be admitted subject to searing cross-examination, and usually discounted by the fact finder because it has insufficient weight to be persuasive.

Examples of Scientist Misconduct

One expert witness, who demonstrated no scientific basis for his opinions, had actually sought out the plaintiff and volunteered his services as an expert.[1] Another of the plaintiff's experts had reached a conclusion as to causation before doing any testing. As one might imagine, their testimony was excluded on the grounds that it lacked probative weight or value.

In another federal court case, the U.S. District Court was presented with an unusual testimonial dilemma.[2] A plaintiff involved in a claim against the Ford Motor Company had modified a vehicle and then obtained expert testimony that the modification had not occurred. The expert witness was aware of the deception but did not disclose it. He was involved in incomplete, dishonest, and misleading reports and testimony. The federal judge handed down a severe censure, resulting in the permanent banning of the expert as a witness in the U.S. District Court.

A number of situations can be envisioned where, because of unsupported or negligent expert testimony, a particular result occurs in the judicial process. In such circumstances, the forensic expert is subject to judicial scrutiny, just like any other professional in a contested setting.[3]

A particularly extreme example of professional ethics abuse is that of Fred Zain, who worked as a forensic scientist in West Virginia and Texas. In a report of the West Virginia Court of Appeals, it was recounted that Zain had:[4]

- Overstated the strength of results and the frequency of genetic matches on individual pieces of evidence
- Misreported the frequency of genetic matches on multiple pieces of evidence
- Reported that multiple items had been tested, when only a single item had been tested; reported inconclusive results as conclusive
- Repeatedly altered laboratory records

- Grouped results to create the erroneous impression that genetic markers had been obtained from all samples tested
- Failed to report conflicting results and failed to conduct or to report conducting additional testing to resolve conflicting results
- Implied a match with a suspect when testing supported only a match with the victim
- Reported scientifically impossible or improbable results

His lies, misrepresentations, and bad science made Zain, who died in 2002, the canonical example of an unethical forensic scientist.

Unfortunately, Fred Zain does not stand alone. A more recent example of fraudulent conduct involves the case of Annie Dookhan. Ms. Dookhan's misconduct led to a multimillion dollar scandal in the criminal justice system. Ms. Dookhan was a chemist working at the Department of Public Health at the Jamaica Plain Hinton Laboratory in Massachusetts. According to a statement by the Massachusetts Attorney General Martha Coakley, Ms. Dookhan was charged criminally with two counts of obstruction of justice and one count of falsely pretending to hold a degree from a college or university. She pled guilty to 17 counts of obstruction of justice, eight counts of tampering with evidence, perjury, and falsely pretending to hold a degree from a college or university. Ms. Dookhan was sentenced to three to five years in prison for her conduct.

Examples of Attorney Misconduct

Unfortunately, attorneys also may attempt to influence the investigation or the opinion of the experts. Attorneys may suppress information or ask loaded or irrelevant questions; on cross-examination, quotations out of context, and hedged facts may be used. The case of the Duke lacrosse team and former Durham District Attorney Mike Nifong's mishandling of that case are just such an example of prosecutorial misconduct. The case centered around charges made by an African American escort and stripper that three members of the Duke lacrosse team, all white males, had sexually assaulted her during a team party where she was performing. The woman later changed her story multiple times regarding the method of attack, the number of attackers, and who the attackers were. During the investigation and subsequently, Nifong:[5]

- Waited six months before he spoke with the "victim"
- Made public a series of accusations that turned out to be false

- Exaggerated and intensified racial tensions
- Unduly influenced the Durham police investigation
- Tried to manipulate potential witnesses
- Refused to hear exculpatory evidence prior to indictment
- Never spoke directly to the alleged victim about the accusations
- Crossed ethical lines by making public comments about the case, possibly prejudicing potential jurors
- Conspired with the DNA lab director to withhold potentially exculpatory DNA

As a result of his conduct, Mike Nifong was disbarred.

In 2013, for the first time in United States Jurisprudence history, a prosecutor was sentenced to jail for failing to disclose evidence. Former prosecutor and then Judge Ken Anderson pled guilty to a single count of criminal contempt for intentionally failing to disclose evidence in the case of *State of Texas v. Michael Morton*. Additionally, as part of the plea agreement, Judge Anderson was forced to give up his license to practice law. While the prosecutor's conduct in that case did not involve expert testimony, it does illustrate how the culture is changing.

Across the aisle, criminal defense attorneys have different questions and different obligations. Criminal defendants are guaranteed certain rights under the United States Constitution, as well as their state constitution. Forensic scientists sometimes wonder:

- Is it proper for an attorney to cross-examine for the purpose of discrediting the reliability or credibility of an adverse witness, when by all appearances, the witness is telling the truth?
- Is it proper to put an expert witness on the stand when you know he will commit perjury? Criminal defendants are constitutionally entitled to a vigorous defense. This includes challenging the witnesses. Areas of challenge for an expert witness may include the witness's truth and veracity; the witness's education, experience, and background; the witness's training; the witness's abilities in other cases; the state of the science; the reputation of the laboratory the scientist works for, just to name a few.

However, despite the criminal defense attorney's obligation to offer a vigorous defense, this does not extend to deliberately suborning the perjured testimony of an expert witness. The rules of professional responsibility are clear to prosecutors, plaintiff's attorneys, and defense attorneys, alike.

Interprofessional Relationships

The American Bar Association published Standards for Criminal Justice. That publication included prosecution and defense standards for dealing with experts. It emphasizes the expert's independence and need for impartiality. The main professional forensic organizations have codes of ethics for their memberships as well. The codes of ethics for the American Academy of Forensic Sciences, the International Association for Identification, the American Society of Crime Laboratory Directors, and the National Commission on Forensic Science (now defunct) are provided below.

American Academy of Forensic Sciences (AAFS)

Article II. CODE OF ETHICS AND CONDUCT

SECTION 1—THE CODE OF ETHICS AND CONDUCT:

As a means to promote the highest quality of professional and personal conduct of its members and affiliates, the following constitutes the Code of Ethics and Conduct which is endorsed by all members and affiliates of the American Academy of Forensic Sciences:

a. Every member and affiliate of the Academy shall refrain from exercising professional or personal conduct adverse to the best interests and objectives of the Academy. The objectives stated in the Preamble to these bylaws shall be to promote professionalism, integrity, and competency in the membership's actions and associated activities; to promote education for and research in the forensic sciences; to encourage the study, improve the practice, elevate the standards and advance the cause of the forensic sciences; to promote interdisciplinary communications; and to plan, organize and administer meetings, reports and other projects for the stimulation and advancement of these and related purposes.
b. No member or affiliate of the Academy shall materially misrepresent his or her education, training, experience, area of expertise, or membership status within the Academy.
c. No member or affiliate of the Academy shall materially misrepresent data or scientific principles upon which his or her conclusion or professional opinion is based.

d. No member or affiliate of the Academy shall issue public statements that appear to represent the position of the Academy without first obtaining specific authority from the Board of Directors.

SECTION 2—MEMBER AND AFFILIATE LIABILITY: Any member or affiliate of the Academy who has violated any of the provisions of the Code of Ethics and Conduct (Article II, Section 1) within the preceding five (5) years may be liable to formal or informal discipline, to include reprimand, censure, suspension, or expulsion by action of the Board of Directors.

SECTION 3—SANCTIONS: If the Board of Directors finds that a member or affiliate has committed a violation of the Code of Ethics and Conduct, the Board may sanction the member or affiliate based on the nature of the violation as follows:

a. If the Board finds that a member or affiliate has committed a minor violation of the Code of Ethics and Conduct, the member or affiliate may be censured with a confidential "Letter of Reprimand" or a non-confidential "Letter of Censure."
b. If the Board finds that a member or affiliate has committed a serious violation of the Code of Ethics and Conduct, the Board may suspend the AAFS membership of the member or affiliate for a specific period of time.
c. If the Board finds that a member or affiliate has committed an egregious violation of the Code of Ethics and Conduct, the Board may expel the member or affiliate from the membership of AAFS.
d. In determining whether a violation of the Code of Ethics and Conduct is "minor," "serious," or "egregious" and appropriate level of sanction to be imposed, the Board of Directors shall consider the following non-exclusive factors:
   1. Whether the violation was an isolated incident or a pattern of misconduct;
   2. Whether the violation was knowing and intentional;
   3. Whether the violation included prevarication, fabrication, deception, or falsification;
   4. Whether the accused has acknowledged the ethical violation, taken remedial measures, and/or expressed remorse for the conduct;
   5. Whether the violation resulted in actual harm or the potential for serious harm to the justice system and/or an individual;
   6. Whether the accused has previously been sanctioned for an ethical violation;

7. Whether the violation involved conduct adverse to the best interests and objectives of the Academy.

International Association for Identification

Code of Ethics and Standards of Professional Conduct

The ethical and professionally responsible International Association for Identification (IAI) member or certificant:

Professionalism

1.01 Is unbiased, and objective, approaching all assignments and examinations with due diligence and an open mind.

1.02 Conducts full and fair examinations in which conclusions are based on the evidence and reference material relevant to the evidence, not on extraneous information, political pressure, or other outside influences.

1.03 Is aware of his/her limitations and only renders conclusions that are within his/her area of expertise and about matters for which he/she has given careful consideration.

1.04 Truthfully communicates with all parties (i.e., the investigator, prosecutor, defense, and other expert witnesses) about information related to his/her analyses, when communications are permitted by law and agency practice.

1.05 Maintains confidentiality of restricted information obtained in the course of professional endeavors.

1.06 Reports to appropriate officials any conflicts between his/her ethical/professional responsibilities and applicable agency policy, law, regulation, or other legal authority.

1.07 Does not accept or participate in any case in which he/she has any personal interest or the appearance of such an interest and shall not be compensated based upon the results of the proceeding.

1.08 Conducts oneself personally and professionally within the laws of his/her respective jurisdiction and in a manner that does not violate public trust.

1.09 Reports to the appropriate legal or administrative authorities unethical, illegal, or scientifically questionable conduct of other practitioners of which he/she has knowledge.

1.10 Does not knowingly make, promote, or tolerate false accusations of a professional or criminal nature.

1.11 Supports sound scientific techniques and practices and does not use his/her position to pressure a practitioner to arrive at conclusions or results that are not supported by reliable scientific data.

Competency and Proficiency

2.01 Is committed to career-long learning in the forensic disciplines in which he/she practices, and stays abreast of new technology and techniques while guarding against the misuse of methods that have not been validated.

2.02 Expresses conclusions and opinions that are based on generally accepted protocols and procedures. New and novel techniques must be validated prior to implementation in case work.

2.03 Is properly trained and determined to be competent through relevant testing prior to undertaking the examination of the evidence.

2.04 Gives utmost care to the treatment of any samples or items of potential evidentiary value to avoid tampering, adulteration, loss or unnecessary consumption.

2.05 Uses controls and standards, including reviews and verifications appropriate to his/her discipline, when conducting examinations and analyses.

Clear Communications

3.01 Accurately represents his/her education, training, experience, and area of expertise.

3.02 Presents accurate and complete data in reports, testimony, publications and oral presentations.

3.03 Makes and retains full, contemporaneous, clear and accurate records of all examinations and tests conducted, and conclusions drawn, in sufficient detail to allow meaningful review and assessment of the conclusions by an independent person competent in the field.

3.04 Does not falsify or alter reports or other records, or withhold relevant information from reports for strategic or tactical litigation advantage.

3.05 Testifies to results obtained and conclusions reached only when he/she has confidence that the opinions are based on good scientific principles and methods. Opinions are to be stated so as to be clear in their meaning.

3.06 Attempts to qualify his/her responses while testifying when asked a question with the requirement that a simple "yes" or "no" answer be given, if answering "yes" or "no" would be misleading to the judge or the jury.

The ethical and professionally responsible International Association for Identification (IAI) member:

Organizational Responsibility

4.01 Does not misrepresent his/her affiliation with the IAI.
4.02 Does not issue any misleading or inaccurate statement that gives the appearance of representing the official position of the IAI.
4.03 Reports violations of this code of which he/she knows to the President of the IAI.
4.04 Cooperate fully with any official investigation by the IAI.

American Society of Crime Laboratory Directors (ASCLD)

Section 2—Code: As members of the AMERICAN SOCIETY OF CRIME LABORATORY DIRECTORS, we will strive to foster an atmosphere within our laboratories which will actively encourage our employees to understand and follow ethical practices. Further, we shall endeavor to discharge our responsibilities toward the public, our employers, our employees and the profession of forensic science in accordance with the following ASCLD Code of Conduct.

2.1 No member of ASCLD shall engage in any conduct that is harmful to the profession of forensic science including, but not limited to, any illegal activity, any technical misrepresentation or distortion, any scholarly falsification.
2.2 No member of ASCLD shall use their position to impose undue pressure on an employee to take technical shortcuts or arrive at a conclusion that is not supported by scientific data.
2.3 No member of ASCLD shall discriminate against any current or prospective employee in his or her organization based on race, color, religion, national origin, sex, age, or disability.
2.4 No member of ASCLD shall engage in any conduct that is detrimental to the purpose of ASCLD as outlined in Article II of the Bylaws.
2.5 No member of ASCLD shall misrepresent his or her expertise or credentials in any professional capacity.
2.6 No member of ASCLD shall offer opinions or conclusions in testimony, which are untrue or are not supported by scientific data.
2.7 No member of ASCLD shall misrepresent his or her position or authority in any professional capacity.
2.8 No member of ASCLD shall make written or oral statements, which imply that the member is speaking on behalf of ASCLD or the Board of Directors without the permission of the President.
2.9 No individual may gain membership in ASCLD nor shall he/she retain membership if they have been convicted of a felony offense.
2.10 All members shall report, to the extent permitted by law, to the Board of Directors any potential ethics violation committed by another member of ASCLD.

The National Code of Professional Responsibility for Forensic Science and Forensic Medicine Service Providers

The National Code of Professional Responsibility ("Code") defines a framework for promoting integrity and respect for the scientific process and encouraging a research-based culture. To increase public confidence in the quality of forensic services, each forensic science and forensic medicine service provider must meet the requirements enumerated below:

1. Accurately represent his/her education, training, experience, and areas of expertise.
2. Pursue professional competency through training, proficiency testing, certification, and presentation and publication of research findings.
3. Commit to continuous learning in the forensic disciplines and stay abreast of new findings, equipment and techniques.
4. Promote validation and incorporation of new technologies, guarding against the use of non-valid methods in casework and the misapplication of validated methods.
5. Avoid tampering, adulteration, loss, or unnecessary consumption of evidentiary materials.
6. Avoid participation in any case where there are personal, financial, employment-related or other conflicts of interest.
7. Conduct full, fair and unbiased examinations, leading to independent, impartial, and objective opinions and conclusions.
8. Make and retain full, contemporaneous, clear and accurate written records of all examinations and tests conducted and conclusions drawn, in sufficient detail to allow meaningful review and assessment by an independent person competent in the field.
9. Base conclusions on generally-accepted procedures supported by sufficient data, standards and controls, not on political pressure or other outside influence.
10. Do not render conclusions that are outside one's expertise.
11. Prepare reports in unambiguous terms, clearly distinguishing data from interpretations and opinions, and disclosing all known associated limitations that prevent invalid inferences or mislead the judge or jury.
12. Do not alter reports or other records, or withhold information from reports for strategic or tactical litigation advantage.
13. Present accurate and complete data in reports, oral and written presentations and testimony based on good scientific practices and validated methods.
14. Communicate honestly and fully, once a report is issued, with all parties (investigators, prosecutors, defense attorneys, and other expert witnesses), unless prohibited by law.

15. Document and notify management or quality assurance personnel of adverse events, such as an unintended mistake or a breach of ethical, legal, scientific standards, or questionable conduct.
16. Ensure reporting, through proper management channels, to all impacted scientific and legal parties of any adverse event that affects a previously issued report or testimony.

Other professional organizations, such as the National Society of Professional Engineers, publish codes of ethics for practitioners.

How to Avoid Abuse

When the system is abused, the players within that system also are abused. Whether it is an O.J. Simpson, a Duke lacrosse team, an exoneration, or the fallout from the allegations in the Reggie Lewis death, the forensic witnesses seem to be in the "middle of the muck." The fallout from either expert witness or attorney misconduct, however, is equally damaging to the system. The remedy for such misdirection is often a matter of knowing one's rights and responsibilities or exercising the proper steps concerning substance or procedure. This section offers an overview and remedies for abuse of and by expert witnesses. The objective of such an examination will hopefully be a more effective, fair, and just resolution of disputes when expert testimony is involved.

As an expert, each time you perform a test, prepare a report, or testify, there is an opportunity to compromise your integrity. While at times this may seem expedient at the moment, the long-term consequences can include unemployment, public disgrace, and even prison time. Employees of government agencies are encouraged to acquaint themselves with the attorney assigned to represent the agency, should they have questions about the proper procedure in a legal matter if they have any questions.

Primary Ethical Issues

Some of the items disclosed and discussed previously center around ethical violations by the forensic witness. However, it might be well to itemize some ethical violations that can occur in the forensic witness arena so they can be avoided.

- Outright false data
- Investigation not performed

- Data altered
- False testimony
- Intentional ignoring of available data
- Recanting prior contra-positions
- Assignments beyond competence
- Accepting unauthorized attorney influence
- Conclusion reached before research
- Conflicts of interest
- Fraudulent credentials

Outright False Data

The cross-examination process is charged with the obligation of exposing falsified information, reports, records, or other basic data. This requires the most meticulous preparation by cross-examining counsel well before the time a fallacious expert takes the witness stand.

Investigation Not Performed

The approach of aggressive counsel includes reviewing the records, reports, bench notes, and protocols to establish that purported investigations were in fact not accomplished.

Data Altered

Resorting to the original documentation is the most effective way of discovering alterations; alterations would be changes to data or documents not supported by analysis. Obliterations through correction fluids, erasures, or digital tampering may be exposed by original document examination. Proper corrections, for example, in the medical field and for forensic laboratory accreditation, require a single line being drawn through a record erroneously made, with the initials of the author. Anything short of that is suggestive of document tampering.

Conditional or Limited Engagement (Private Experts)

On occasion an expert will be conditionally engaged by counsel, only to have the undertaking terminated before any work is accomplished. The scope of engagement should be revealed through the expert's file. It would be unethical for an expert to tender opinions beyond the scope of the engagement.

False Testimony

On occasion, a witness will falsely testify based upon information either erroneously provided or carelessly gathered. Rarely false testimony arises from an intentional desire on the part of the witness to support the claim of the sponsoring party with no regard for the truth or falsity of the statement. Here the anvil of cross-examination provides strength for the opposition.

Ignoring Data

This oversight can occur through counsel or client who would not reveal to the expert all requisite data, or by the expert turning a professional cold shoulder on salient facts. In either case, a cross-examination may expose such blindsiding.

Recanting Prior Contra-Positions

Often an expert has testified to or written concerning a particular proposition. The diligent cross-examiner who uncovers a prior contra-position in another related or similar case has, in hand, the tools to send the expert "to the showers." Be mindful of what you say on the witness stand, understanding that those statements may come back to haunt you. If you have a legitimate reason for changing your position, be sure you can document your reasons for doing so.

Assignments Beyond Competency

This area of cross-examination often goes not to admissibility of expert testimony, but rather to the weight given to an expert's testimony. An expert clearly out of depth should be so exposed by careful cross-examination that indicates the assignment was simply beyond the witness's experience and capability.

Unauthorized Attorney Influence

Communication between expert and attorney is the best way to uncover efforts by sponsoring counsel to influence the professional expert opinions. Normally such correspondence is not privileged in any way except if it is pure attorney work product and was not relied on by the expert in forming a professional opinion. In the event the witness has relied in whole or in part on the attorney statement, such information is proper for production and examination.

Reaching Conclusions Before Research

One of the delightful opportunities for cross-examining attorneys is to have an expert jump to a conclusion before any study or research has been done to buttress or support the conclusion. Through cross-examination and meticulous file analysis, it is often possible to uncover the fact that an expert opinion or conclusion was reached before any research was done. This likewise goes most often to weight and not admissibility. If the circumstances are sufficiently egregious, it may be that the witness's entire testimony will be stricken.

Conflict of Interest

Conflicts of interest can provide a legal basis for expert challenge and a court-ordered disqualification of an expert witness. In the event materials were made available to an expert on the other side of an assignment, prior to the current assignment, there is case law that will prohibit an expert from testifying in the current case. Aside from circumstances that justify disqualification, a conflict of interest situation presents a viable area of cross-examination that may go to the weight of the testimony and really impinges on the expert's integrity.

Fraudulent Credentials

Here, the task is prediscovery: Checking details of an expert's curriculum vitae and personal resume. While experts are admonished to maintain a careful recitation of historic accomplishments, some tend to exaggerate their own credentials. By verifying the data contained in the resume prior to trial, it is possible to expose the expert to outright falsehoods in the resume. Falsehoods in the resume obviously lead the fact finder to a conclusion there are falsehoods in the report as well.

Contingent Fee (Private Experts)

Obviously if an expert's compensation is driven by a contingency outcome, witness credibility and weight given to such testimony are highly suspect. If an expert reveals a compensation formula that is contingent on case outcome, serious doubt can be cast on the veracity and credibility of such an expert witness.

Abuses of Experts

The following conduct represents a non-exhaustive list of conduct an attorney should not engage in:

- Inquiry into personal and individual finances (unless that inquiry could relate directly to bias or partiality)
- Threats by attorney concerning possible contempt of court or sanctions for not answering questions, unless you are being intentionally evasive
- Refusal to allow the physical setting and circumstances of the deposition room to be comfortable for you
- Not permitting reasonable breaks in the proceeding for fatigue or physical comfort
- Counsel continually asking repetitive, argumentative, redundant, or insignificant questions for purposes of "wearing down" expert
- Examining attorney engages in badgering or overly aggressive questioning techniques
- Unreasonable time demands placed on expert for preliminary or final report
- Seeking "expert opinion" without affording any opportunity for expert to explore data, inspect premises, do testing, or otherwise investigate the matter
- Expert is not provided access to key underlying information
- Witness pushed to render opinions beyond limits of engagement
- Expert asked to opine in areas beyond witness's expertise
- Expert contacted by opposite party without notice to retaining attorney
- Expert asked to perform analysis on the stand
- Expert expected to, or instructed to, make findings consistent with attorney's theory of case
- Expert asked to testify without adequate deposition or pretrial preparation
- Inquiry into private life or habits that embarrass, humiliate, intimidate, or harass expert (drugs, alcohol, sexual practices, etc.) where the questions do not relate to competency or impeachment and have no bearing on expert's ability or effort as an expert witness

Abuses by Experts

- Interrogatory responses not updated and made current by experts
- Expert did not disclose all opinions intended to be rendered as required by pretrial order
- Expert violated some other order of the court
- Expert withheld information
- Destruction of evidence in testing
- "Consulting" expert volunteers to testify against the side hiring him
- Expert tenders false credentials
- Expert renders untrue opinion or report
- Expert tenders opinion based on "vast experience" only, without doing any real scientific, technical, or professional investigation
- Witness generates long, rambling preamble to every question
- Expert takes on an assignment that will involve disclosure of confidential information received from the opposite party in an earlier matter

Asserting Your Rights as a Witness

You have the right not to be abused as an expert testifying witness, either in trial or deposition. Abuse of an expert witness may be subtle or direct. Of course, sponsoring counsel has some obligation to keep the examination on proper course. You may ask sponsoring counsel what procedures will be followed if abusive questioning is encountered.

There are many devices available to you for self-protection. You may benefit from knowing what to do in such an emergency. An answer such as "I really think that is an abusive question" should probably do the job to alert the attorney you think the line of questioning is becoming aggressive. However, this response should be reserved for extremely rare circumstances.

Above all, refuse to engage in shouting matches or arguments with abusive attorneys or in response to convoluted or incomprehensible questioning. Be aware of how your comments, answers, or objections might look in print. Know your rights and be ready to exercise them, but do not fire too quickly from the hip.

A forensic witness's credibility can be severely attacked if a lack of documentation for the basis of their testimony is shown. Often the quantum of evidence gathered by the expert is inadequate to establish the particular causation for which the witness has been called to testify.

If experimental evidence is generally insufficient to support the witness's conclusion, such testimony will be elicited during cross-examination to erode the believability of the forensic witness. The prepared cross-examiner will know this inadequacy prior to taking on the expert. While there may be some support for the expert witness's testimony in scientific, technical, or professional literature, if the support is of a minimal nature or generally undocumented, or if the support comes from discredited spokespersons, all of those items go to the weight and lack of reliability that would attach to the tendered witness.

Sometimes an expert witness will testify to a conclusion and will not rule out alternative causes of the condition that may have created the circumstance. The skillful expert will eliminate each and every alternative cause. The inadequately prepared expert may not be able to know these are areas of vulnerability on cross-examination.

Aggressive cross-examination may reveal the expert did not rely on proprietary or regulatory standards of agencies to support the conclusions tendered. To the contrary, if there are relevant standards, either industry-wide or promulgated by government entities, and if the testimony does not comport with those standards, major headway is made in the cross-examination process.

Countering the Claim of Junk Science

The phrase "junk science" has been popularized by an author who may himself have been, in the opinion of some legal scholars, guilty of doing junk research to write about junk science. In any case, the phrase has highlighted elements of inadequate forensic testimony that create a good checklist for cross-examiners to follow as they address a supposedly inadequate, incompetent, or unprofessional forensic witness.

There are a variety of approaches an attorney may take with their expert to address an opposing witnesses' use of junk science. Show the witness is just not knowledgeable on the subject. Expose lack of meticulous attention to detail that the expert witness failed to follow in preparation. Cross-examine as to lack of activity in the professional field, particularly with regard to absence of current education and training and lack of appropriate seminar and workshop attendance. Whenever possible, the cross-examining attorney should avoid allowing his expert to recognize the charlatan as an "expert." Establishing that the witness has never testified to the same effect previously is damning cross-examination. If the cross-examiner can establish the findings of the witness are not consistent with studies of others, credibility of the testifying witness is seriously eroded. If cross-examination suggests that the expert's findings often lead to erroneous results, the expert's credibility is again jeopardized.

Often an expert will indicate that present methods are positively related to prior methodology. If that linkage and connection can be dispelled, the weight of testimony and credibility of the witness are threatened. The witness should be pressed for literature that tends to support the testimony. Absence of such literature bolsters the claim of lack of competence and credibility. If tests or examinations conducted by the forensic expert have never been admitted as evidence in a court or other dispute resolution process on previous occasions, such lack of admission seriously questions the validity of the extant testimony. The aggressive cross-examiner will often show there is no government regulation or statutory support for the expert testimony, or that the expert testimony is simply not approved either by the scientific community or any government-sponsored methodology. If the cross-examining attorney can establish the scientific, technical, or professional community does not rely on the same tests, procedures, or techniques followed by the expert, a serious erosion of the expert witness's testimony occurs. To state these issues in a positive format, the expert must:

- Be a knowledgeable professional
- Be meticulous with detail
- Be active in the field as well as an expert witness
- Show you have testified to the same effect previously
- Show your findings are consistent with studies by others
- Show your findings seldom lead to erroneous results
- Prove new methods are positively related to prior methods
- Identify literature that establishes your approach
- Show prior admission of these same tests in other cases
- Relate your tests to the same type of tests by the opposition
- Show approval of your methodology through published standards
- Establish the scientific community's reliance on these same tests

Conclusion

Statements of ethical behavior often sound preachy or strident. Ethical behavior, however, is what makes or breaks your reputation. To end on a positive note, the correlative of each of the negatives contained in this chapter should provide ample warning to the careful forensic witness and sponsoring attorney as to methods and procedures to be used to avoid these kinds of attack based upon fraudulent, unethical, or improper conduct by the expert.

The objective is always to improve the quality of the criminal justice system, not trap or trick the serious and dedicated forensic witness who is attempting to assist the judicial system in resolving disputes.

Review Questions

1. What are ethics?
2. What are normative ethics?
3. Name three codes of ethics from AAFS.
4. Name three codes of ethics from IAI.
5. Name three codes of ethics from ASCLD.
6. Name three codes of ethics from another forensic professional organization.
7. Name three codes of ethics from one organization that does not appear in another's.
8. Name three primary ethical issues.
9. What is the best way to prevent witnesses from using fraudulent data?
10. State five ways you can be an ethical expert.

Discussion Questions

1. Why are ethics so important? Can ethics be learned later in life or are they set through your upbringing?
2. Why do you think the ethical codes of various organizations vary? What does this say about ethics?
3. What is the best way to deal with unethical behavior, either yours or others? How should a laboratory deal with unethical behavior of its employees?

Notes

1. Socha, C.Q., "Excluding Plaintiff's Expert Testimony," *For the Defense*, September 1987, p. 24.
2. *Schimdt v. Ford Motor Company*, 112 F.R.D. 216 (D. Cob. 1986).
3. See, for example, Restatement (Second) Torts, §299 A (1965); *Bruce v. Byrne-Stevens & Associates*, 51 Wash. App. 199, 752 p.2d 949 (1988), revised 776 p.2d 666 (1989), was just such a case. The court concluded that experts are

not immune from claims when they do their work in a negligent manner. The Supreme Court of Washington, in reversing the lower appellate court, based its decision on the doctrine of testimonial immunity.

4. West Virginia Court of Appeals, No. 21973, "In the Matter of an Investigation of the West Virginia State Police Crime Laboratory, Serology Division," November 4, 1993.
5. Neff, J., "Lacrosse Files Show Gaps in DA's Case," *The News & Observer*, August 6, 2006.

Preparing for the Future 10

Key Terms

Artificial Intelligence (AI)
Confrontation Clause
Smith v. Arizona
Surrogate analyst
Deepfakes
Black box problem
Virtual reality (VR)
3D-printed firearm
Ghost gun
Recycled materials
Green materials
Federal Analogue Act

Introduction

The recent amendments to Federal Rule of Evidence (FRE) 702, discussed earlier in this book, emphasize that expert testimony may only be admitted if the court determines "that it is more likely than not that the proffered testimony meets the admissibility requirements set forth in the rule," and are only the beginning of the changes expert witnesses will be seeing soon. The future of expert testimony is likely to be significantly shaped by technological advancements and evolving legal standards, particularly regarding the use of Artificial Intelligence (AI) and virtual reality (VR) in the courtroom. There will be an increased emphasis on transparency and reliability of expert opinions, and experts may need to adapt to new formats and procedures. While the new FRE 702 places a greater burden on the proponent to demonstrate the reliability and validity of the expert's opinion, the inevitable use of AI in expert testimony will necessitate clearer disclosures about its application, ensuring reliability and avoiding the pitfalls of AI hallucinations or fabricated information.

DOI: 10.4324/9781003610540-10

The Sixth Amendment and Testifying for Another Expert

The Sixth Amendment to the U.S. Constitution guarantees every criminal defendant the right "to be confronted with the witnesses against him." This protection, known as the Confrontation Clause, plays a critical role in how forensic science is presented in court, particularly when it comes to expert testimony. Forensic experts and laboratories must be acutely aware of the legal and ethical implications of this constitutional guarantee, especially in situations where one expert is asked to testify based on the work performed by another.

Surrogate Testimony and the Supreme Court's Stance

In the landmark case *Smith v. Arizona*, the U.S. Supreme Court addressed a recurring issue in modern forensic practice: Whether one expert can testify in place of another who actually conducted the testing. The Court ruled that a "surrogate analyst" cannot introduce out-of-court statements made by a non-testifying analyst, even if those statements are presented as the basis of the surrogate's own expert opinion. The decision reaffirmed the principle that defendants have the right to cross-examine the actual analyst whose work is being offered as evidence.

This ruling has significant implications for forensic laboratories. In a small lab, one analyst may handle multiple aspects of a case, such as sampling, testing, interpreting results, and even writing the report, so the individual who testifies is the same person who performed the work. But in larger laboratories, duties are often divided among multiple personnel for efficiency. One analyst may prepare the samples, another may run the instrument, and a third may interpret the data. Under *Smith v. Arizona*, each of these contributors could, in theory, be required to testify if their work forms part of the evidentiary foundation.

Operational and Ethical Dilemmas

The *Smith* decision poses a practical dilemma for laboratories: Should they continue with an efficient division of labor that maximizes throughput, or revert to assigning single analysts to entire casework packages, knowing that cross-functional work may trigger confrontation issues in court?

There are also ethical considerations. If one analyst presents conclusions based on data they did not generate or personally verify, and the original analyst is unavailable for cross-examination, the defense is denied a meaningful opportunity to challenge the quality, context, or interpretation of the foundational work. Even when well-intentioned, such proxy testimony risks undermining both due process and the credibility of forensic science as a discipline. Moreover, experts who testify based on another's work without sufficient familiarity may find themselves on ethically shaky ground. They may inadvertently make assertions they cannot fully defend or explain. This places the expert witness in conflict with their duty to provide honest, unbiased, and scientifically supported testimony.

Laboratory Policy Implications

Laboratory management must account for these legal realities when designing workflows, retention policies, and staffing models. Policies should anticipate the possibility that any individual who performed a critical function in a forensic analysis may be called to testify. This includes planning for staff turnover, retirements, and other departures, as analysts can still be subpoenaed years after leaving an agency. Requiring documentation that clearly traces who did what and when in a case file is not only good quality assurance, it is essential for legal defensibility.

Some labs have begun to update their standard operating procedures to address this issue directly. For example, analysts are often required to review and sign off on their contributions in ways that clearly document their role. In some cases, all contributors to an analysis may be listed in the report, not just the final author. This can help ensure that the correct individuals are identified for testimony and reduce the risk of inadvertent Sixth Amendment violations.

The dilemma is not theoretical. Laboratory decisions that prioritize efficiency at the expense of individual accountability may expose forensic evidence to exclusion, especially if the court determines that a defendant's right to confront the actual analyst has been denied. While some jurisdictions have allowed limited exceptions or encouraged stipulations to ease this burden, such practices cannot replace the foundational guarantee of the Confrontation Clause.

Ethically, laboratories must take care not to create systems that implicitly encourage the use of surrogate testimony to maintain case throughput. Doing so may shift risk onto analysts, undermine public trust, and ultimately erode the integrity of the justice system. As the American Civil Liberties Union cautioned, courts should resist balancing "bedrock procedural guarantees" against alleged system efficiencies.

The Sixth Amendment's Confrontation Clause places a clear responsibility on forensic laboratories and expert witnesses: Evidence introduced in court must be accompanied by testimony from those who actually performed or directly supervised the analysis. Surrogate testimony—no matter how well-intentioned—may violate a defendant's rights and jeopardize a conviction. Experts must therefore be vigilant in understanding the limits of their own knowledge and avoid venturing beyond the bounds of what they can credibly and ethically support in court. Laboratory managers, meanwhile, must develop policies that respect both the demands of forensic casework and the constitutional rights of the accused.

Artificial Intelligence

AI is poised to reshape the way forensic science is practiced and presented in courtrooms. At its core, AI refers to a broad range of computer systems that perform tasks typically requiring human intelligence—such as recognizing patterns, making predictions, or interpreting language. In forensic science, AI can analyze massive datasets, enhance images, detect anomalies, or even model complex events based on incomplete evidence. But AI doesn't testify. People do. And this distinction lies at the center of a growing concern among judges, attorneys, and forensic experts alike.

In March 2025, the Federal Judicial Conference's Advisory Committee on Evidence Rules proposed an important change: The creation of a new Rule 707 of the FRE. If adopted, this rule would require courts to treat AI-generated evidence by the same standards already applied to human experts under Rule 702. That means the party introducing AI-based results, like the output of a predictive algorithm, biometric match, or statistical reconstruction, must show that the system used reliable methods, was appropriately applied to the facts, and produced valid results.

The underlying issue is reliability. Machine learning systems, especially deep learning models, can be extremely complex and often opaque. They can't be cross-examined. They may not offer explanations that human jurors or judges can understand. This raises questions that mirror those long asked of human experts: Can the methods be reproduced? Are the underlying assumptions valid? Is the output specific and accurate, or is it the result of overfitting, bias in training data, or software design choices that no one in the courtroom fully understands?

The proposed Rule 707 is not intended to stifle innovation. It makes room for emerging tools by asking proponents to do what they should already be doing: Demonstrate the basis and reliability of their evidence. For example, if a party introduces a facial recognition result generated by an AI system, they must be able to explain how the system works, what data it was trained on, and whether its error rate is acceptable for the stakes of the case.

This proposed change builds on a broader legal reckoning with machine-generated evidence. Judges have already begun pushing back against AI output that lacks transparency. In *Z.H. v. New York City Department of Education*, a court rejected ChatGPT-generated legal claims due to a lack of identifiable inputs and unreliable citations. Other courts have expressed concern about AI-enhanced video or audio evidence, especially where the expert couldn't verify how the AI tool had modified the data. The challenge isn't just about expert evidence, it's also about authentication. Courts are starting to grapple with deepfakes: Videos, images, and audio recordings that may be partially or entirely AI-generated. A separate proposal to amend Rule 901 would give judges more explicit authority to exclude evidence if there's a reasonable basis to believe it was fabricated by AI, unless the proponent can prove it is more likely than not authentic. Making all this more problematic, even the people who create AI don't understand how it knows what it knows. Sam Altman, the CEO of OpenAI, acknowledged that the company hasn't "solved interpretability" when asked about the internal workings of their large language models (LLMs) during a summit in June 2024. This means the AI models' outputs and decisions aren't fully understood, representing a "black box" problem where the internal logic is unclear. If the creators don't understand it, how will you, as the expert who used it in a technical sense, be able to explain what it did?

While this language has not yet been adopted, the mere fact that the federal judiciary is considering it signals a critical shift: AI is not just another forensic tool; it's a potential witness whose presence must be justified under the same standards as any human expert. For the forensic expert, these developments underscore the importance of understanding the tools used in their analysis. If you use an AI system, you may need to explain not only what it did, but how it did it and why that's a trustworthy basis for your conclusions. You cannot defer responsibility to the software, because in court, the software cannot speak.

Whether courts ultimately adopt Rule 707 or rely on existing Rule 702 standards, one principle remains constant: The goal is not to keep out new technology, but to ensure that any evidence, no matter how impressive it may seem, is based on sound science and clearly explained to those who must rely on it.

Virtual Reality and the Courtroom

Technological innovation has never been a stranger to the courtroom. From crime scene photography in the nineteenth century to 3D laser scanning today, forensic scientists have long relied on visual aids to help explain complex evidence to judges and juries. Now, with the advent of VR, expert witnesses may be on the brink of a new frontier in evidentiary presentation. Virtual reality refers to computer-generated, immersive environments that simulate real or imagined worlds. With a headset, a user can be virtually transported to the middle of a crime scene, walk through the trajectory of a bullet, or examine the positioning of forensic evidence from multiple angles. Unlike two-dimensional diagrams or videos, VR offers the potential for participants to experience spatial relationships directly, which may enhance comprehension and retention.

Proponents of VR in the courtroom suggest it could be a game-changer for expert testimony. Instead of describing a reconstruction, an expert can guide jurors through it, helping them to "see" rather than simply imagine what the scene looked like. For example, in a vehicular accident case, a traffic collision reconstructionist might use VR to let jurors virtually ride along in one of the vehicles, offering a unique perspective on sightlines, obstructions, and timing.

But while the technology is promising, the use of VR in court raises legal and ethical challenges that experts must be prepared to navigate. One concern is whether VR simulations constitute demonstrative or substantive evidence. Demonstrative evidence is designed to aid understanding but does not stand on its own as proof; substantive evidence, by contrast, is offered as factual. If a VR simulation introduces interpretive elements, such as estimated speeds or missing details filled in by the creator, courts may scrutinize its admissibility more closely under rules governing scientific evidence.

Accuracy and fairness also come into play. A virtual environment that exaggerates blood spatter size, overemphasizes a defendant's proximity to a weapon, or uses dramatic lighting can unconsciously influence jurors. VR simulations, like any other expert aid, must be grounded in the physical evidence and reflect the limitations of the underlying data. Forensic experts have a duty to clearly explain what the simulation is based on, what assumptions were made, and what elements were approximated or omitted. It is well known that eye witness testimony is highly unreliable, so what happens when the jury become meta eye witnesses?

Finally, there are also logistical considerations. Not all courts are equipped with the necessary VR hardware. Access to the same immersive experience must be provided to all parties in a case, including the prosecution, defense, judge, and jury. This may require significant coordination, training, and budgetary resources, factors that can vary widely from one jurisdiction to another.

As of this writing, courts are beginning to experiment with VR on a case-by-case basis. In one California case, a forensic pathologist used a virtual autopsy reconstruction to support conclusions about cause of death. In another, German prosecutors created a VR model of Auschwitz to assist in trying aging war criminals. Each case has helped refine the standards and protocols for admissibility, but consensus remains elusive. For forensic scientists, the lesson is clear: VR is not science fiction anymore. While not yet commonplace, it is emerging as a tool that may reshape how experts communicate complex information in court. Those who choose to adopt it must treat it with the same rigor they apply to any other scientific method: Validating the input data, documenting the reconstruction process, and explaining limitations transparently. If used responsibly, VR could offer jurors not just a better view but a deeper understanding of the evidence that matters.

Emerging Technologies and Forensic Science

Forensic science doesn't operate in a vacuum. It is embedded in the larger ecosystem of human activity, and that activity is increasingly driven by rapid technological change. From the street corner to the lab bench, new tools and techniques are shaping not only how crimes are committed but also how they must be investigated. Some of these technologies arrive with fanfare; others appear in evidence bags before courts have ever heard of them. The field of forensic science must adapt to each in turn.

3D-Printed Firearms and the Rise of the "Ghost Gun"

One of the most disruptive technologies to enter forensic caseloads is the 3D-printed firearm, colloquially known as a "ghost gun." These weapons are often manufactured using commercially available 3D printers and polymer materials, assembled from modular components, and notably lack serial numbers. Without traditional manufacturing marks, they fall outside most regulatory frameworks, making them difficult to trace. Even more challenging, parts can be produced separately, in private homes, and combined into fully functional firearms with minimal technical knowledge.

From a forensic standpoint, ghost guns complicate traditional firearm identification. Examiners typically rely on toolmarks left by factory equipment to link a firearm to a batch, manufacturer, or even a particular weapon. With 3D-printed guns, the surface characteristics are shaped by a digital file and a home printer's quirks rather than factory tooling. That means examiners must rethink what "individual characteristics" mean in this context and often must analyze inconsistencies introduced by printing artifacts, wear on polymer components, or hybrid construction using parts from different sources.

Courts have also begun to grapple with these challenges. Is a 3D-printed receiver equivalent to a factory receiver for purposes of firearm classification? Can the presence of a digital file be considered intent to manufacture? These are legal questions, but they hinge on scientific clarity. As the technology becomes more accessible, forensic laboratories will be called upon to evaluate and explain its implications clearly and accurately.

Recycled and "Green" Materials: A New Class of Synthetic Evidence

Another frontier lies in materials science. Recycled plastics, textiles made from mixed-source fibers, and biodegradable composites are increasingly common in consumer goods—and, by extension, in forensic evidence. While these innovations support environmental goals, they introduce complexity for evidence analysis. A single garment may now contain cotton, regenerated cellulose, polyester, and bioplastic threads spun together in proprietary weaves, often indistinguishable by traditional microscopy.

Such complexity doesn't just affect fiber analysis. Trace materials, such as microplastics or synthetic adhesives, may originate from unknown or custom-manufactured sources, challenging efforts to classify them or determine origin. The more diverse the input materials, the harder it becomes to make meaningful comparisons or to offer confident conclusions about significance. As the market evolves, forensic scientists must stay ahead of the manufacturing curve, investing in broader spectral libraries, improved classification algorithms, and new reference databases tailored to hybrid materials.

In this context, "green" doesn't always mean easier or safer. Some biodegradable materials begin to decompose under ordinary storage conditions. Others leave minimal residue, making them harder to detect. The forensic significance of a trace may shift not because the science has changed, but because the materials themselves are now ephemeral or deliberately engineered to leave no trace.

AI-Driven Illicit Drug Design

Perhaps the most unsettling technological development facing forensic chemistry is the emergence of AI in illicit drug design. AI models, many of them developed openly for pharmaceutical research, can now be repurposed to generate molecular structures that do not yet exist in public databases. The result is a wave of synthetic drugs with no formal name, no established toxicity profile, and no predictable effect beyond their biochemical similarity to known psychoactive substances.

This phenomenon is sometimes referred to as "designer drugs by design," and it marks a shift in how forensic toxicologists must approach their work. Traditional drug identification relies on libraries of known spectra and targeted screening protocols. But if the compound doesn't exist in any database, those tools offer little help. Instead, laboratories may need to invest in untargeted screening techniques—high-resolution mass spectrometry, molecular networking, and rapid metabolite prediction—to even begin to make sense of the unknown compound.

The legal system, likewise, struggles to keep up. In the United States, the Federal Analogue Act allows prosecution of substances that are "substantially similar" to controlled drugs, but the interpretation of similarity (whether structural or functional) isn't always clear-cut. Forensic experts may be asked to testify not only about what a compound is, but what it could be used for, how it was likely synthesized, and whether it is likely to produce effects similar to Schedule I or II substances. That places a heavy research burden on laboratories, which must now interface with frontier pharmacology, computational chemistry, and policy interpretation.

In each of these examples—ghost guns, green materials, AI-designed drugs—the common thread is that the boundary between "technological innovation" and "forensic evidence" is increasingly thin. Experts are no longer simply keeping up with criminals; they are keeping up with entire industries, global research pipelines, and digital ecosystems that develop faster than case law or quality assurance systems can respond. As new forms of evidence emerge, forensic science must not only adapt its methods, but anticipate how these tools will be used, misused, and contested in the courtroom.

Conclusion

Expert testimony is evolving in response to legal developments and technological change. The recent amendment to Federal Rule of Evidence 702 signals a shift in how courts evaluate expert opinions, placing greater emphasis on reliability and requiring proponents to demonstrate that their testimony meets admissibility standards. This heightened scrutiny is likely to expand with proposed Rule 707, which would apply similar standards to AI-generated evidence. As expert witnesses, students should be aware that relying on advanced tools, especially those they cannot fully explain, may limit the credibility or admissibility of their conclusions.

The constitutional implications of surrogate testimony under the Sixth Amendment are significant. The U.S. Supreme Court's ruling in *Smith v. Arizona* reinforced a defendant's right to confront the analyst who performed or directly supervised forensic testing. This ruling has practical consequences for laboratory workflows and expert testimony. Experts must be prepared to testify only to their own work and avoid making claims based on evidence they did not directly analyze.

Finally, the growing role of emerging technologies such as VR, 3D-printed firearms, recycled materials, and AI-designed synthetic drugs, will have an impact on expert testimony. Each of these technologies presents new challenges for forensic science, from authentication and classification to courtroom presentation. As future forensic professionals, students must be prepared not only to understand how these tools work, but also to explain their methods, assumptions, and limitations clearly and accurately. As the tools of science evolve, so too must the expert's responsibility to ensure that evidence is communicated transparently and ethically.

Review Questions

1. What does the recent amendment to Federal Rule of Evidence 702 require of expert witnesses and the parties that introduce their testimony?
2. Why did the U.S. Supreme Court rule in *Smith v. Arizona* that surrogate analysts cannot testify in place of the original examiner?
3. How does the Confrontation Clause of the Sixth Amendment apply to forensic expert testimony in criminal trials?
4. What are the potential legal and ethical risks when an expert testifies to conclusions based on another analyst's work?
5. What operational changes might a forensic laboratory consider to comply with *Smith v. Arizona* and ensure testimony is constitutionally sound?
6. What is the purpose of the proposed Federal Rule of Evidence 707, and how would it affect the use of AI-generated outputs in court?
7. Explain why AI tools present challenges in expert testimony, especially regarding transparency, interpretability, and reliability.
8. How might VR be used in expert testimony, and what are the evidentiary concerns that accompany its use in court?
9. Why do 3D-printed firearms, or "ghost guns," complicate traditional forensic firearm analysis and legal regulation?
10. How are new synthetic materials and AI-designed drugs changing the expectations and methods of forensic analysis in laboratories today?

Discussion Questions

1. Should forensic laboratories prioritize efficiency in case processing, even if it increases the likelihood of surrogate testimony? Why or why not?
2. As AI becomes more embedded in forensic workflows, what responsibilities do experts have in understanding and explaining the tools they use?
3. How might the use of VR in courtrooms enhance or hinder a jury's understanding of forensic evidence? Where should the line be drawn between illustration and influence?
4. With technologies like 3D-printed firearms and designer drugs developing faster than laws can keep up, what role should forensic scientists play in shaping policy and legal standards?
5. Do you think the legal system is equipped to handle the complexities introduced by AI-generated evidence? What changes, if any, would you propose to ensure fairness and reliability?

Index

Note: Page references with "n" represent note numbers.

D

E

N

O

P

R

S

T

For Product Safety Concerns and Information please contact our EU
representative GPSR@taylorandfrancis.com
Taylor & Francis Verlag GmbH, Kaufingerstraße 24, 80331 München, Germany

www.ingramcontent.com/pod-product-compliance
Ingram Content Group UK Ltd.
Pitfield, Milton Keynes, MK11 3LW, UK
UKHW020206200926
475702UK00004B/631
* 9 7 8 1 0 4 1 0 0 5 7 5 9 *